Praise for the Football School series

"Hilarious ... packed with amazing football facts, cartoons, jokes."
The Week Junior

"Will spark a love of learning in any child who reads it... Intelligent, inspiring, funny."
Head of Education, Premier League

"We love this book series!"
Match of the Day Weekly

"A dream for young footie fans."
The Sun

"Funny, informative and hugely entertaining."
BookTrust

To Bonzo – A.B.

To ABC & M, with love – B.L.

For my constant studio companions, Freddie & Biscuit – S.G.

First published 2019 by Walker Books Ltd
87 Vauxhall Walk, London SE11 5HJ

This edition published 2020

2 4 6 8 10 9 7 5 3 1

This book has been typeset in Palatino

Printed and bound by CPI Group (UK) Ltd, Croydon CR0 4YY

British Library Cataloguing in Publication Data:
a catalogue record for this book is available from the British Library

ISBN 978-1-4063-9293-7

WALKER BOOKS

FSC
www.fsc.org
MIX
Paper from responsible sources
FSC® C020471

www.walker.co.uk

www.footballschool.co

FOOTBALL SCHOOL

Season 4

WHERE FOOTBALL ~~EXPLAINS~~ celebrates THE WORLD

ALEX BELLOS & BEN LYTTLETON

Illustrated by Spike Gerrell

Welcome to Football School Season 4!
Hi, everyone. I'm Alex.
And I'm Ben. We're your teachers.
Coaches! Because every lesson here is about football.
Yes! We believe that football is the best way to celebrate our wonderful world.
You will be learning, laughing ...
... and loving it!
To start, we are salivating to tell you the story of saliva.
You'll be spitting with rage to miss it!
We are counting the minutes until we explain how referees tell the time.
Peep! Peep!
We can't wait to introduce you to some amazing characters, like the oldest goal-scorer in the world...
And a woman born a thousand years ago who fans still remember today!
AB
BL

We will sing the praises of the man who uses classical music to improve his players.
Turn it up!
And we'll do a one-two with the genius who invented shirt numbers.
Three-sy does it!
We'll learn about monkey bottoms in Nigeria.
Cheeky!
And travel to the country where the national kit is based on a chessboard.
Check-y!
Our Star Pupils are excited to get to know you.
And you'll find quizzes at the end of each lesson. Careful, though! The cartoons do not always illustrate the correct answer.
We would also like to invite you to the first ever Football School Magic Club.
You'll learn some tricks to stun your friends, both on the pitch and off it.
Absolutely! Because reading this book will make you a smarter footballer.
Sounds like magic to me!
Let's go!
AB
BL

MEET YOUR COACHES

ALEX "BELLINHOS" BELLOS

Coach Stats

Birthplace: Oxford
Favourite film: Toy Story
Favourite vegetable: Aubergine
Favourite fruit: Mango
Favourite time of the day: When I wake up
Favourite sock colour: Blue with red dots
Match I'd love to watch live? Brazil v. Argentina
Favourite spot to watch match: From the halfway line
Favourite coach: Marcelo Bielsa
Fashion role model: Carlos Valderrama
Alphabet five-a-side Dream Team (A–E): Alisson, Bronze, Charlton, De Bruyne, Eriksen

Coach Stats

Birthplace: London
Favourite film: Bugsy Malone
Favourite vegetable: Spinach
Favourite fruit: Pineapple
Favourite time of the day: Just before kick-off
Favourite sock colour: Pink
Match I'd love to watch live? Boca Juniors v. River Plate in Argentina
Favourite spot to watch match: Behind the goal
Favourite coaches: Thomas Tuchel, Emma Hayes
Fashion role model: Dani Alves
Alphabet five-a-side Dream Team (V-Z): Van der Sar, Wan-Bissaka, Xavi, Yankey, Zidane

BEN "THE PEN" LYTTLETON

TIMETABLE

	MONDAY	TUESDAY
REGISTRATION		
LESSON 1 LESSON 2	BIOLOGY 10–23	MUSIC 52–65
LESSON 3 LESSON 4	MODERN LANGUAGES 24–35	COMPUTER SCIENCE 66–79
LUNCH	1.00–2.00PM	
LESSON 5	MATHS 36–51	PHILOSOPHY 80–93

Find the answers to the quizzes on page 200. But no cheating!
BL

Monday
Lesson 1+2

BIOLOGY

Lick your lips everyone, we're going to start the day with a celebration of saliva!

Saliva is a marvellous liquid and it has many uses, from dissolving our food to cleaning our teeth.

It is also frequently seen flying out of footballers' mouths.

In this lesson we'll ask why players are so keen to fire gloopy globules from their gobs. We'll look at some of the most notorious spitters in the game and we'll find out about the soup that is made entirely from saliva!
Slurp slurp!

Are you spitting – sorry, sitting – comfortably? Then let's get the juice about drool!

SALIVA LIVE OH

Let's start by thinking about the most delicious cake you have ever eaten in your life. Remember how the soft sponge pressed on your tongue and the icing melted in your mouth. Mmmmm.

As you think about that cake, are you noticing a build up of saliva under your tongue? The thought of your favourite food is usually enough to activate the saliva glands in your mouth.

These glands are tiny holes that squirt out saliva. You can find them under your tongue, near the back of your throat and in the sides of your cheeks. If you pass your tongue around the inside of your cheek, you should be able to feel a small lump on either side. That's a **saliva duct**. By now, with so much thinking about saliva, your mouth should be full of it. No spitting in class, though!

Humans are saliva-producing machines: an adult will easily produce two pints of it every day. Cheers!

SUPER SALIVA

Saliva is a miracle substance with many uses. For a start, it's the best and cheapest oral hygiene treatment around. Did you know that saliva performs the following four vital functions in the mouth?

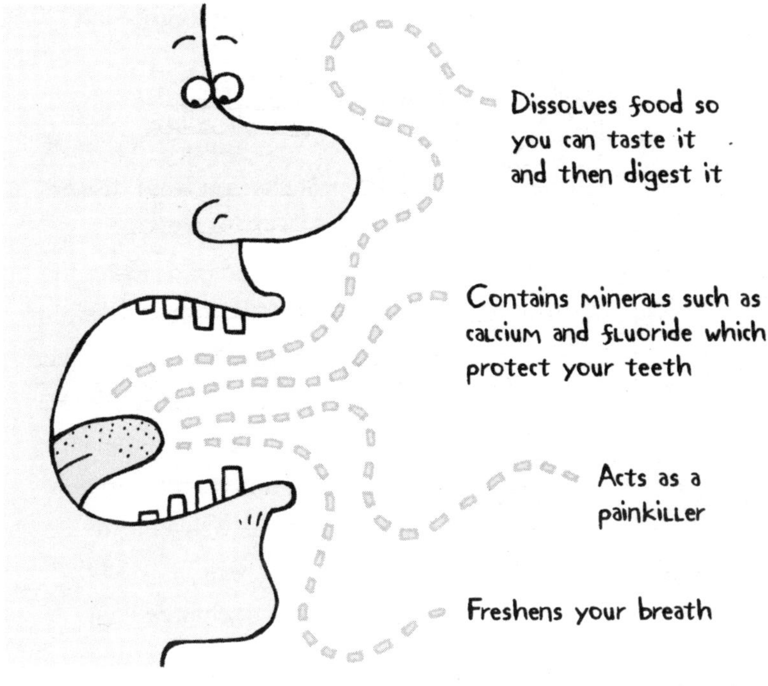

In fact, the stinky breath we wake up with in the morning is the result of a lack of saliva during the night. Morning breath is caused by bacteria lingering in the mouth. Saliva contains chemicals that kill bacteria. When we are sleeping, however, saliva production drops, causing the bacteria in our mouths to thrive, resulting in fragrant morning breath. Yuk – pass the toothpaste!

FOOTBALL DROOLS THE WORLD

Saliva contains secrets about your health, which is why lots of clubs regularly test their players' saliva. The doctors are looking for many different chemicals, including:

- **Cortisol:** a chemical that indicates how stressed you are.
- **Testosterone:** a chemical related to your aggression levels.
- **Immunoglobulin A:** a substance which has nothing to do with gobbing or goblins. It's an important part of your immune system, which protects you from disease.

If a player's saliva sample shows a ratio of testosterone to cortisol that is much lower than normal, it could be an indication that he or she is over-training. If the immunoglobulin A levels are down, this will make them more prone to infections. These red flags will alert the team doctor, who may advise the player to change their training routine.

Testing a player's blood would reveal similar information. But clubs often prefer to test saliva, since asking a player to drool into a tube or swab their tongue is faster and more convenient than taking blood with a needle.

GOB JOBS

Footballers are well known for spitting on the grass during breaks in play. Athletes in other sports like rugby, tennis, cycling and gymnastics rarely spit. So we spoke to saliva experts, sports scientists and players to find out why footballers can't resist shooting liquid out of their mouths. We learned that:

SLIPPERY CHARACTERS

Footballers are allowed to spit on the pitch, even if it is a bad habit. To spit on another person, however, is absolutely forbidden. In the Premier League, the offence gets you a mandatory six-match ban.

El Hadji Diouf

When El Hadji Diouf was playing at Liverpool, he spat at a Celtic fan during a match between the two teams and ended up in court. He pleaded guilty to the charge of assault and was fined £5,000. Liverpool also fined him two weeks' wages and he was banned for two games.

Fabien Barthez

France goalkeeper Fabien Barthez's greatest moment was winning the 1998 World Cup, but his worst moment was being banned for six months in 2005 for spitting at a referee. The incident happened in a very unfriendly friendly between his club side Marseilles and Wydad Casablanca that descended into a brawl.

Frank Rijkaard

In a bad-tempered second-round match between the Netherlands and West Germany in the 1990 World Cup, German Rudi Voller and Dutchman Rijkaard were both sent off. As they walked to the touchline, Rijkaard spat a thick globule of spit that lodged in Voller's hair. It was one of the most famous incidents in World Cup history, for all the wrong reasons.

SPIT SPORT

If you love to eject things from your mouth, why not try these sports. Several competitions require you to spit an object as far as possible. Let's take a look at what people are spitting around the world – but maybe don't try this at home!

CRICKETS

Devised by a zoologist to promote understanding of insects, the crickets must be frozen and thawed before being placed in the mouth for the spit. The world record is 9.77m.

WILD SPITTING

Many animals rival footballers as champion spitters! Here are Football School's favourites:

SALIVA IN MY SOUP

Bird's nest soup is a Chinese delicacy that is made from bird spit. The swiftlet, a type of bird from the Asia-Pacific region, makes its nest from solidified saliva. For hundreds of years the Chinese turned these nests into soup, which they believe is nutritious, delicious and good for your skin.

TARGET MAN

The archerfish shoots its prey by squirting water from its mouth, just like when Alex fires at Ben with a water pistol. The fish swims just below the surface and when it sees a tasty-looking insect, it spits a jet of water at it. The insect then falls into the water to be guzzled by the fish. Archerfish can spit accurately at an insect from 2 metres away, which is especially amazing since a jet of water does not travel in a straight line, but in a curved path pulled down by gravity.

LLOVELY!

If you see a llama looking anxious, with its ears pulled back flat and making a gurgling sound, then duck! It is probably about to spit at you. These cuddly South American mammals can spit up to nearly 5 metres with very good accuracy. Llamas, however, only spit when they are scared, or fighting, or showing who is the stronger animal. Usually they are peaceful and friendly. But when they do spit ... well, it's mostly vomit: stinky and green and originating in one of the animal's three stomachs.

SPITTOON ARMY

Spitting is not socially acceptable in the present day, but in the eighteenth and nineteenth centuries it was a perfectly normal thing to do. Homes and public places like pubs would have small bowl-like receptacles, called spittoons, for people to spit into. This practice mostly stopped about a hundred years ago when doctors realized that spit could carry diseases.

BIOLOGY QUIZ

1. **Which of these does saliva do?**

a) Washes your hair
b) Ties your shoelaces
c) Tucks in your shirt
d) Cleans your teeth

2. **When doctors test saliva for signs of overtraining, what substance are they looking for?**

a) Chewing gum
b) Cortisol
c) Plaque
d) This morning's breakfast

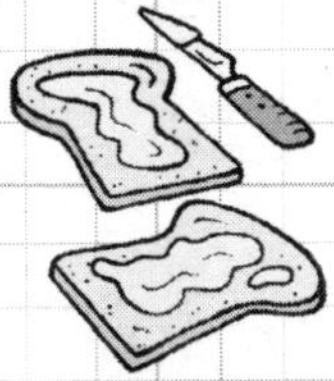

3. **The world record for spitting a piece of kudu dung is 15.56m. The kudu, which lives in South Africa, is a type of?**

a) Antelope
b) Giraffe
c) Elephant
d) Sheep

4. **Which artist said: "If I spit they will take my spit and frame it as great art"?**

a) Leonardo da Vinci
b) Pablo Picasso
c) Damien Hirst
d) Banksy

5. **What does the phrase "a spitting image" mean?**

a) Someone who looks exactly like someone else
b) A rain cloud
c) A painting made out of spit
d) A portrait of an angry llama

Monday
Lesson 3+4

MODERN LANGUAGES

Hold your horses! We're going on a global tour in this lesson to learn football phrases from around the world. We call this the *ABCD (WXYZ)*, or *Alex and Ben's Classroom Dictionary (Wildlife X-amples for Young Zoologists)*, because all the entries involve animals. Whether you are a fan in France, a commentator in Kenya or a nut in Brazil, it seems that if you want to talk football you need to pay attention to what slithers, crawls, swims and flies.

Animal phrases are an example of how a creative use of words increases our enjoyment of the game, whatever language you speak. When we compare something that happens on the pitch to something that happens in the animal kingdom, we are painting a picture in our minds that is more exciting, colourful and funny. We could, of course, compare football to anything, but animals work particularly well because we are familiar with them (except for snakes, hopefully!) and because they are living things with distinctive, memorable features. These phrases make us laugh like hyenas! We think they're the bee's knees!

Aile de pigeon •
Means: Pigeon wing
From: France
Language: French
A back-heel when a player bends their leg behind or beside them. The angle of the leg to the heel looks like a pigeon's wing. Just don't back-heel the bird!

Atet nkura •
Means: Hiding mice
From: Ghana
Language: Twi
Strikers who operate inside the penalty area but don't like to do any defensive work are said to be mice hiding in the box, as mice are timid creatures.

Bal yapmayan ari •
Means: Bee without honey
From: Turkey
Language: Turkish
Used to describe a player who runs around a lot but doesn't bring that much to the team, or a hardworking team that has no end result.

Bubamara •
Means: Ladybird
From: Bosnia and Herzegovina
Language: Bosnian
This was the original Bosnian nickname for the black-panelled Adidas ball used at the 1970 World Cup. It is now used to describe any football. Ladybirds are seen as a good-luck charm in Bosnia.

Buffelstoot •

Means: Buffalo header
From: Belgium
Language: Flemish

This term describes a dominant header that cannot be stopped. It stuck after a reporter used the word to describe a headed goal scored with power and strength – a funny choice since the only buffaloes in Belgium live in the zoo.

Culebrita •

Means: Little snake
From: El Salvador
Language: Spanish

A trick that forwards use to beat their markers. This requires a player to use their toes to quickly pass the ball between their own feet before dribbling around the outside of the defender. The speed of the change of direction outwits all but the sharpest defenders – and the wiggle of the ball's direction replicates that of a slithering snake. Jorge "Mágico" González, the star of the El Salvador national team in their World Cup appearance in 1982, perfected this trick in both directions.

Curi ayam •

Means: Stealing chickens
From: Malaysia
Language: Malay

Strikers who play on the edge of the offside rule, always making a nuisance of themselves around the area, are said to be stealing chickens. This Malay phrase is used to describe people who do things in an underhand way. Not to be confused with *kaki ayam*, which means chicken foot and refers to anyone playing football barefoot.

Drible de foquinha •
Means: Seal dribble
From: Brazil
Language: Portuguese
When a Brazilian teenager called Kerlon invented a new way of dribbling with the ball, it made headlines across the world. Kerlon's technique involved scooping the ball from the ground to his head, and running while juggling it on his head – similar to the way a trained seal, with head up and nose aloft, can balance a ball on its nose. It was almost impossible to tackle Kerlon without conceding a foul – this was a seal-ly special trick!

Gajah sepakbola •
Means: Elephant football
From: Indonesia
Language: Malay
When elephants play football, as some do for tourists in Thailand and Indonesia, they tend to charge around trying and failing to kick the ball. This was likened to the way two teams played in a controversial second division match in Indonesia in 2014 when both of them, PSS Sleman and PSIS Semarang, were trying to lose. The final score was 3–2, and all five goals scored were own goals. Both teams were disqualified and their coaches banned from football for life.

Geomi-son •

Means: Spider-hands
From: South Korea
Language: Korean

In South Korea, a goalkeeper who keeps everything out is known as a spider-hands. The original *geomi-son* was former Russia keeper Lev Yashin, who was nicknamed the Black Spider. South Korea goalkeeper Lee Woon-jae, who was selected for four World Cups, was also nicknamed *geomi-son*.

Kampfschwein •

Means: Battle pig
From: Germany
Language: German

A complimentary phrase used to describe a tough-tackling midfielder who is not afraid to get stuck in and make hard challenges. Snortttt!

Kukanyaga nyoka •

Means: Step on a snake
From: Kenya
Language: Swahili

Used to describe what happens when you try to strike the ball in the air and miss. It looks as though you are jumping in the air after treading on a snake. Kenya is home to over 100 species of snake so Kenyans need to watch their steps! Not to be confused with a *piga ngoma kimo cha bafe*, a puff adder shot, which is a shot struck low that whizzes along the ground, just like an adder.

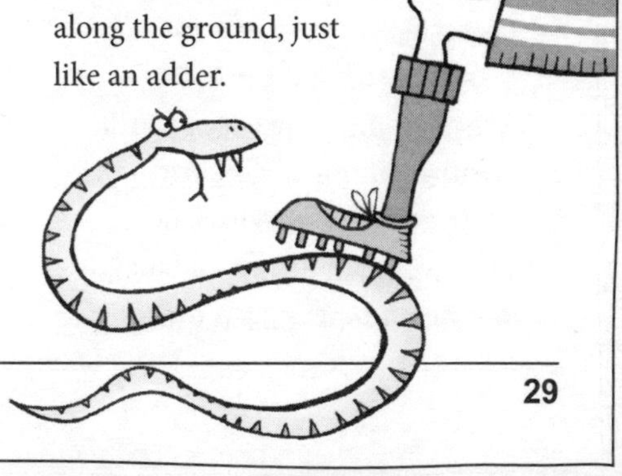

Lepkevadász •

Means: Butterfly hunter

From: Hungary

Language: Hungarian

A goalkeeper whose attempts to gather crosses look like someone trying, but failing, to catch butterflies.

Makrellfotball •

Means: Mackerel football

From: Norway

Language: Norwegian

This term was coined in honour of the IK Start team who were crowned Norwegian league champions in 1978 and 1980. Start is based in the port city of Kristiansand, close to the North and the Baltic Seas. The core of the team had played together in the youth academy, and they knew each other's movements so well that the team in full flow resembled a shoal of fish. A team that plays perfectly in sync is said to play *Makrellfotball* – smells fishy to us!

Monkey yansh •

Means: Monkey bottom

From: Nigeria

Language: Ig

A brightly-coloured bruise that you get from falling over on a particularly bumpy or hard pitch, so it resembles the bright bottom of a monkey.

Onde dorme a coruja •

Means: Where the owl sleeps
From: Brazil
Language: Portuguese

This is the very top corner of the goal, where an unstoppable shot might end up. No goalkeeper can stop a shot going in *onde dorme a coruja*. The Spanish version is *donde anidan las aranas*, or where the spiders nest, while in Trinidad it's *jep nest*, or the wasp's nest.

Palomita •

Means: Little pigeon
From: Argentina
Language: Spanish

A goal scored with a diving header, as though a pigeon is flying through the air. The most famous in Argentina dates back to 1971, when Aldo Poy scored for Rosario Central. Over 40 years later, Rosario fans still celebrate his *palomita* by recreating it with Poy on the day of the goal's anniversary. In Brazil, this is a *gol de peixinho*, a little fish goal.

Papegøjespark •
Means: Parrot kick
From: Denmark
Language: Danish
A shot struck with the outside of the boot is known as a parrot kick, because the curve that the ball normally takes resembles the shape of a parrot's beak.

Schwalbenkönig •
Means: King of the swallows
From: Germany
Language: German
This term is used to describe a player who executes the perfect dive in order to win a penalty or free kick. The *schwalbe*, a swallow, is the chosen bird because it flies low to the ground and has long wings that look similar to a player's waving arms as they fall to the ground.
All hail the *Schwalbenkönig*!

Táctica del murciélago •
Means: Bat tactics
From: Ecuador
Language: Spanish
A team defending close to its own goal-line is thought to resemble a row of bats hanging upside down from the crossbar.

Timsaha yatmak •
Means: Doing a crocodile
From: Turkey
Language: Turkish
Getting ahead of yourself, for example by celebrating before the final whistle has blown. The expression dates back to 2010, when Fenerbahçe fans thought they had beaten Bursaspor to the Turkish league title on the final day of the season. The Bursaspor team are nicknamed the Green Crocodiles and the Fener fans mocked them by doing a crocodile walk, marching on their knees and grabbing the ankles of the person in front. But Fenerbahçe's celebrations turned out to be premature and unwarranted because Bursaspor went on to win the title. Awkward!

Yaseed hamaam •
Means: To hunt pigeons
From: Saudi Arabia
Language: Arabic

When a shot goes flying over the crossbar and disturbs the birds in the roof of the stadium.

BIRD ON THE WING

The best ever player to have an animal nickname was Garrincha. The Brazilian winger was named after the garrincha, a little bird that looks a bit like a wren. He was one of the world's best dribblers, despite – or perhaps because of – the fact he was born with two bent legs. Garrincha played alongside Pelé and won the World Cup in 1958 and 1962. Indeed, he was so talented that once a referee sent him off for dribbling too much!

MODERN LANGUAGES QUIZ

1. What language is spoken in Brazil?

a) Brazilian
b) Spanish
c) Portuguese
d) Twi

2. What does the German word "schwein" mean?

a) Pig
b) Buffalo
c) Snake
d) Crocodile

3. What animal phrase is used in England to describe a striker who always snaps up chances to score from close range?

a) Foal with a goal
b) Fox in the box
c) Pet in the net
d) Horse who scores

4. "Caballo" means horse in which language?

a) Japanese
b) French
c) Croatian
d) Spanish

5. What animal has the largest eyes in the world, each one about the same size as a football?

a) Blue whale
b) Giant squid
c) Wild camel
d) Karma chameleon

Monday
Lesson 5

MATHS

Stop the clocks! This afternoon we're concerned with how numbers divide the day. It's about time!

What's the first thing that happens in a game of football? The referee checks his watch and blows his whistle. One of the ref's most important jobs is as a timekeeper, making sure that a game is made up of two halves of 45 minutes, with some time added on for injuries. In the next few pages, we'll be looking at the history of time measurement. We'll discover where the idea for hours, minutes and seconds came from, and we'll check out the latest in referees' timepieces.

Synchronize your watches, it's lesson o'clock!

ABOUT TIME

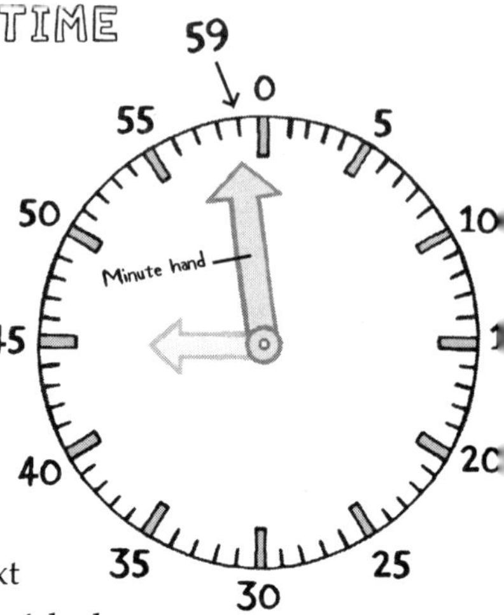

Here's a simple maths question. What number comes after 59?

You might think that the answer is 60. Usually, it is. But not always.

When it comes to counting time, the number after 59 is 0.

If a clock says 1.59 p.m., which means 59 minutes past one in the afternoon, the next number will be 2.00 p.m., or two o'clock.

Likewise, if your stopwatch says 3mins 59secs, the next number is 4mins 0secs.

If you think about it, it really is quite strange that there are sixty seconds in a minute, and sixty minutes in an hour.

Why not 70, or 80, or even 100?

The reason we count time in units of 60 is because a civilization from about six thousand years ago decided this would be a good idea. The **Mesopotamians** lived in the Middle East, roughly where Iraq is now. Let's go back in time to the ancient world.

SIXTIES OBSESSION

The Mesopotamians were the first people in the world to have a **system of numbers**, meaning a set of words and numerals for numbers. Before them no one was able to say "I have five fingers" or "100 per cent" or even "I beat you 1–0." Instead they would have said something like "I have a hand's worth of fingers", or "totally" or "I scored more than you."

Introducing number-words and numerals meant that farmers could say exactly how many goats they had, a system of **money** could be developed and parents could finally count their children. Phew! Numbers helped turn Mesopotamia into the first great civilization.

The numbers they used, however, were different from the ones we use today. They preferred to count in groups of 60. No one knows for definite why they chose this number, but it might be because it's easy to do sums with. For example, 2, 3, 4, 5, 6, 10, 12, 15, 20 and 30 all divide into 60. Neat!

TINY SLICES

As well as counting in groups of 60, the Mesopotamians also divided things into 60. They divided the circle into 60 equal parts.

Each of these parts became known as a *minute* part, because they were really, really tiny. This is where the word minute comes from.

To create an even smaller unit of measurement, each minute part was then divided into 60, into a *second minute* part, which is where the word second comes from.

This way of dividing the circle worked so well that no one has changed it in six thousand years. The Mesopotamian number system was rejected by later civilizations for one that counts in groups of 10, but when it comes to minutes and seconds, this ancient system has – literally! – stood the test of time.

THANKS A DOZEN

The Mesopotamians invented minutes and seconds. The next great advance in time measurement came from another ancient civilization, the **Egyptians**, who lived four thousand years ago. Famous for pyramids, hieroglyphics and mummies, the ancient Egyptians were also the best time-measurers of their age.

Egyptians told the time using the sun. They built a tall stone pillar and watched the shadow of the pillar move slowly across the ground as the sun changed position in the sky. By looking at where the shadow was at any moment during daylight, they could tell the time. Interestingly, this is exactly how a later invention, sundials, also work. Many churches and other historic buildings have them.

The Egyptians divided the period of daylight into 12. Again, no one knows why they decided on 12. One explanation is that 12 is divisible by 2, 3 and 4, which means that the maths is easy if we want to divide the daytime into halves, thirds and quarters. Whatever the reason, the 12 caught on, and this is why we have 12 hours on a clock face, and why there are 24 hours in the day.

WATCH OUT

As well as using the sun and shadows, the ancient world used other methods to measure time, such as hourglasses, candles and water clocks based on water dripping at a constant rate. With the invention in the fifteenth century of mechanical clocks with clock faces and hands, based on a wind-up system of springs and cogs, the noise of measuring time went from drip-drip to tick-tock.

Within a few hundred years craftsmen had figured out how to make cogs, gears and springs that were small enough to fit in a palm-sized device, enabling them to build the first pocket watches. At first they were quite heavy, but eventually watches became light enough to wear on the wrist.

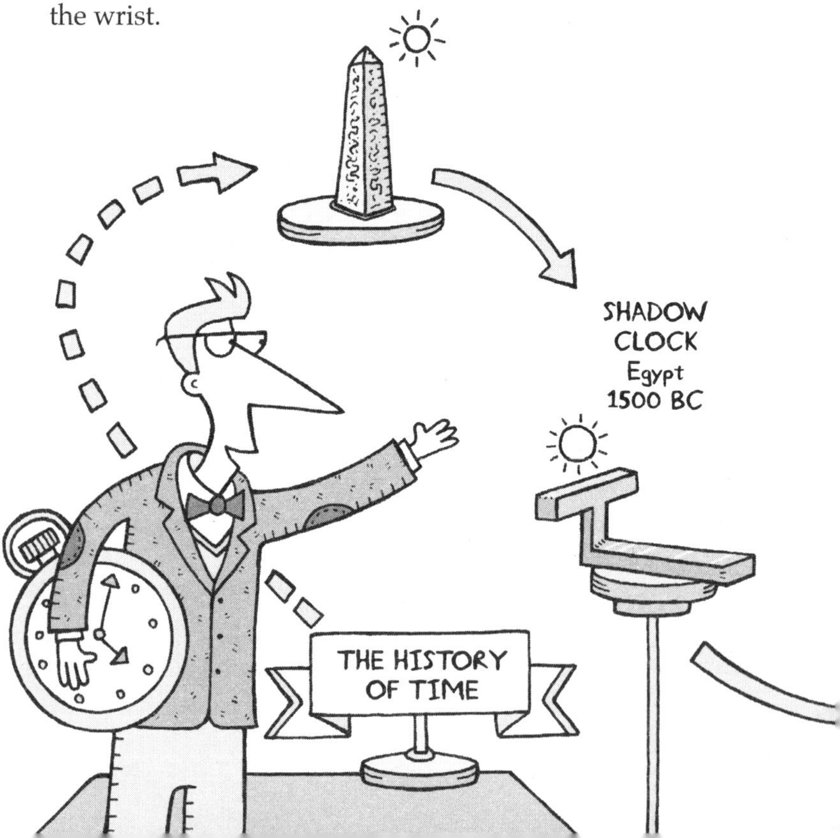

Today we no longer have to wind our watches because most are electronic. They work using quartz crystals: a battery sends an electrical signal to a tiny piece of rock called quartz, which vibrates and produces a regular electronic pulse. The pulse powers a motor that moves clock hands, or, if the watch is digital, connects to a numerical display. We hope that's crystal clear!

The watches worn by Premier League referees, however, are smartwatches, meaning they are small computers in watch form. The watch face is a touch screen. Referees don't need to wind them up or even put batteries in them. They just need to remember to charge them before games!

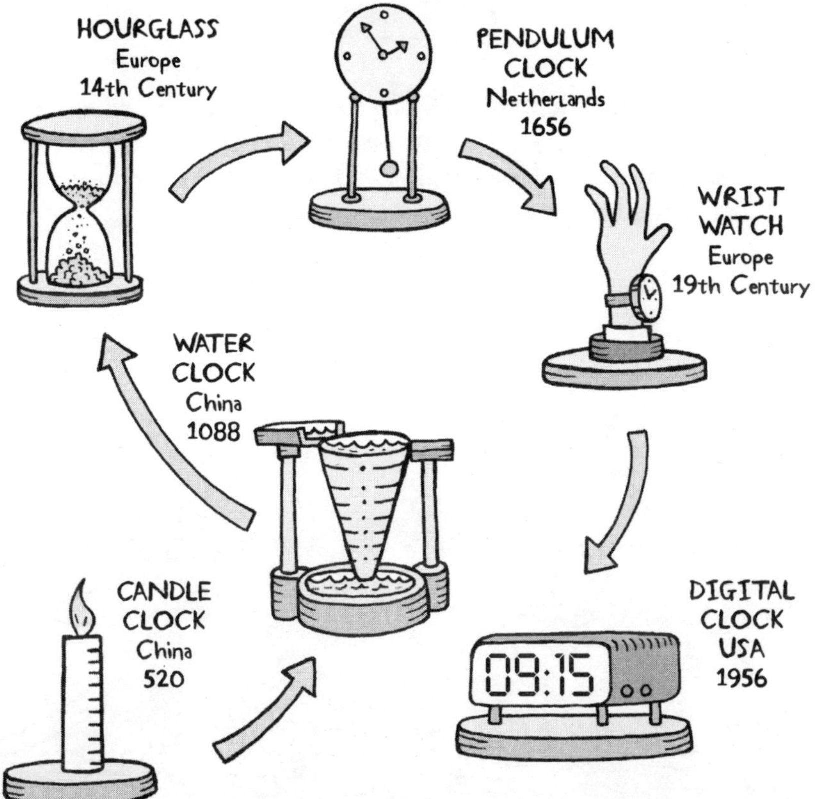

WATCH CLOSELY

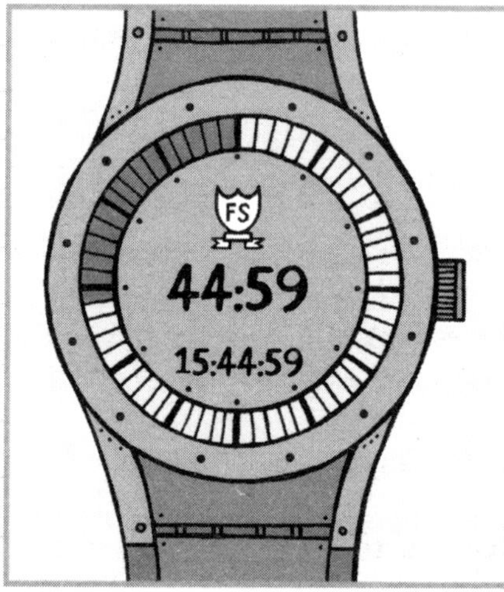

It's a referee's job to make sure the game starts on schedule, as clubs may get fined if the match starts late. It needs to end on time too. Here's a peek at the latest Premier League watch, and how the refs use it to keep time.

1. The 4-digit number in the middle is a timer. It starts at 00:00 and counts the minutes and seconds of the game. The 6-digit number at the bottom shows the time of day.

2. The timer keeps running even if play is stopped for injuries or non-game related reasons (such as the floodlights failing). A fourth official (the reserve referee) makes a note of how long the stoppage lasts, and shortly before the end of the half informs the referee via headset how many extra minutes are to be allocated.

3. After 45 minutes, the watch vibrates.

4. During stoppage time a green segment around the edge of the watch lights up each minute so it is easy for the ref to know how many minutes have been played. Once the extra minutes have been played, the referee whistles to mark the end of the half.

5. In the second half the timer starts at 45:00.

A GAME OF THREE THIRDS

Football matches have lasted 90 minutes since the origins of the game in the nineteenth century. The earliest recorded match dates back to 1866, when there was no break for half-time. Oof! In 1897, the FA officially ruled that matches must last 90 minutes in the Laws of the Game. The rules also said that half-time should not exceed 5 minutes, unless the ref consented to longer. That's barely enough time to go to the loo!

Football is the only major sport with a 90-minute game. It is fascinating that of the sports below – all team sports that use balls – none of them divide their matches in the same way. Sports that are faster and more physical have shorter games so as not to exhaust the players. Poor lambs!

SPORT	LENGTH OF MATCH	BREAKS
Rugby	80 minutes	Two halves of 40
Hockey	70 minutes	Two halves of 35
American football	60 minutes	Four quarters of 15 minutes
Ice hockey	60 minutes	Three 20-minute periods
Basketball	48 minutes	Four quarters of 12 minutes
Beach soccer	36 minutes	Three 12-minute periods

BALL TIME

In football, the match clock keeps on ticking when the ball is not in play, such as when the goalkeeper is holding the ball before a goal kick, or when a player is waiting to perform a throw-in. If you were to count up the time the ball is in play, this averages at somewhere between 50 and 60 minutes per match. In some matches the ball is in play for less than 50 minutes – meaning that for almost half the 90 minutes, there is no football to watch. Bo-ring!

In recent years, football's authorities have started to think about changing the time-keeping rules in order to make sure fans are guaranteed the full amount of football. One suggestion is that a football match should consist of two halves of only 30 minutes, but that these 30 minutes are "playing time", which means that the clock stops whenever the ball goes out of play and starts again when play recommences. This way of time-keeping is already used successfully in rugby union, American football and basketball, where it ensures that all matches have exactly the same amount of action.

By counting only playing time, you would get rid of gamesmanship, such as when players walk very slowly to the touchline when being substituted, or when they spend ages taking a corner in order to run down the clock without giving the ball away. The game would become fairer. We think it might work well. Time's up for time-wasters!

GONE WITH THE WIND

The fastest goal of all time according to the FA took only 2 seconds. Blink and you missed it! The goal was scored in an amateur game between Cowes Sports and Eastleigh in the Wessex League. Marc Burrows put the ball on the centre spot, saw that the keeper was off his line and took a shot, which went in thanks to the wind.

One of the fastest goals in professional football is believed to have been scored after 3.17 seconds, by the Brazilian Fred, in 2003, playing for Brazilian club América Mineiro against Vila Nova.

MATHS QUIZ

1. Which country is where Mesopotamia used to be?

a) India
b) Israel
c) Iraq
d) Egypt

2. How many minutes are there in a day?

a) 360
b) 720
c) 1,440
d) 86,400

3. In a football match, if the clock shows that 3 minutes and 10 seconds have elapsed, which minute of the game are we in?

a) Second
b) Third
c) Fourth
d) Fifth

4. How many minutes are in a sixth of a game of football?

a) 12
b) 15
c) 18
d) 20

5. What is a gnomon?

a) A toadstool with a clock
b) A gnome with a watch
c) A long white beard that tells the time
d) The piece in a sundial that casts the shadow

Tuesday
Lesson 1+2

MUSIC

A surge of strings! A fanfare of trumpets! A rousing chorus of voices!

At Football School we love music. We listen to modern musical styles like pop, rock and rap. But we also love **classical music**, the old-fashioned type of music played by orchestras using instruments like the violin, the cello, the flute, the clarinet and the kettledrum.

In this chapter we will discover what football can learn from classical music. We'll meet a famous coach obsessed with the composer Vivaldi, hear about the 300-year-old piece of music that still gives players goosebumps and learn about the great composer who wrote one of the world's first football songs. If you want to get the low-down about the double bass, try your pluck with the harp or have a hoot with the flutes, tune in now!

Music, Maestro!

GOOD CONDUCT

Classical music is the name given to a type of music that emerged in Europe in the seventeenth century, partly as a result of the invention of modern musical notation. Once composers were able to write down music that could easily be read, they began to write grand pieces for **orchestras**, collections of up to around 100 musicians led by a conductor wielding a small stick, or **baton**. (Previously, music was performed by small groups.) Depending on the structure of the music, classical pieces were given names like **symphony**, **concerto** and **sonata**. Famous composers include Mozart, Bach and Brahms.

So far, so good, sonata! But what has this got to do with football? Quite a lot, as it happens. Think about it:

- An orchestra is a collection of talented individuals directed by a single person, the conductor, who stands in front of them and tells them what to do by waving their hands about.
- A football team is also a collection of talented individuals directed by a single person, the coach, who stands on the touchline and tells them what to do by waving their hands about.

Italian classical music buff Giovanni Trapattoni was always comparing the role of the conductor of an orchestra to a football coach. And he should know, since he was one of the best coaches in history. Trap won ten league titles in four different countries: for Juventus in Italy, Bayern Munich in Germany, Benfica in Portugal and Red Bull Salzburg in Austria. Let's find out more about this maestro of the pitch.

TRAP MUSIC

Trapattoni has classical music in his blood. He was born only a few miles from La Scala, the opera house in Milan and one of the most famous classical music venues in the world. As well as learning to play football as a child, Trapattoni played the French horn, a brass instrument which you blow through a mouth piece, then the air goes round a circular tangle of pipes before coming out of the bell at the end. Perrp, perrp!

As a player at AC Milan in the 1960s, Trap won two Serie A titles and two European Cups (that's the forerunner of the Champions League). But as well as collecting silverware he also started collecting classical music. He has an enormous collection that supposedly runs to more than 2,000 records.

Trapattoni spent a lot of time comparing his two greatest loves and came to the following conclusions:

DO! In an orchestra the most important lesson is teamwork and thinking collectively. You need to make sure that the musicians are working together with a common goal.
If one musician is playing off-key, or too loudly, it ruins the experience for everyone! Likewise, football is a team sport. If one player is ignoring a team-mate in a better position, or showboating (showing off) on a solo dribble, the team will suffer.

RE! The conductor directs the musicians by setting the speed and the rhythm of how the piece is played.
Likewise, in football players can learn about building attacks by varying the speed and movement of the game.

MI! The conductor's role is to encourage, improve and inspire – just like the role of a football coach. And both conductors and coaches have to know how to manage divas!

Trap believes that classical music made him a better player and person. He urged his players to explore the work of composers like Schubert and Beethoven. "Whoever listens to Mozart can play football better," he said. Sing it loud, Trap!

EAR WE GO

If you want to improve your football by listening to classical music, we recommend beginning with Trap's three favourite pieces:

Composer: Antonio Vivaldi
Work: Four Seasons
Date: 1721
Nope, he wasn't writing about the football seasons! Vivaldi expresses each season of the year through music.

Composer: Franz Schubert
Work: Seventh Symphony
Date: 1821
Schubert only sketched out this symphony, which was completed after his death.

Composer: Ludwig van Beethoven
Work: Ninth Symphony
Date: 1824
One of the most performed symphonies in the world, Beethoven was almost totally deaf when he composed it.

CLASSIC POWER

Trapattoni is not alone in thinking that classical music improves wellbeing. Scientists have discovered that classical music can decrease our heart rate, which makes us more relaxed. It is also said that people who fall asleep listening to classical music sleep better. But not during training!

THE ORCHESTRA XI

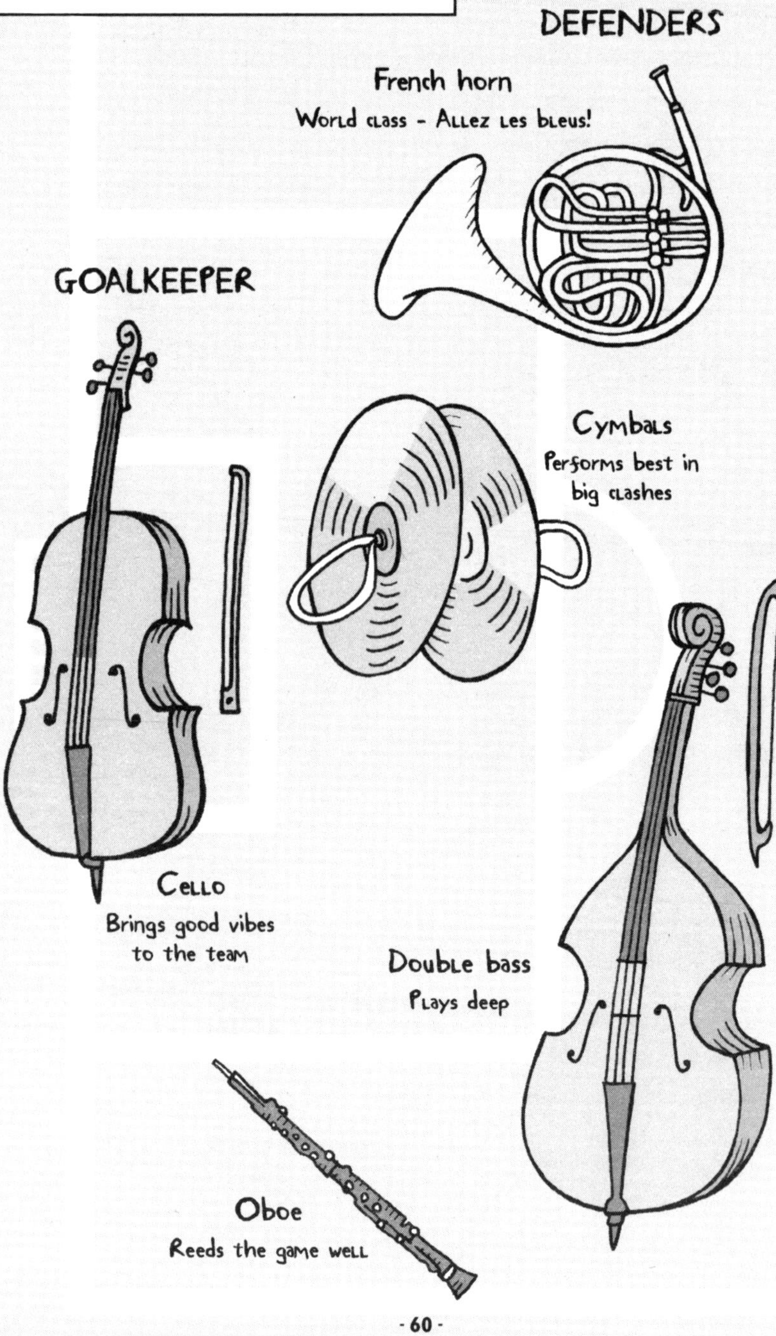

MIDFIELDERS

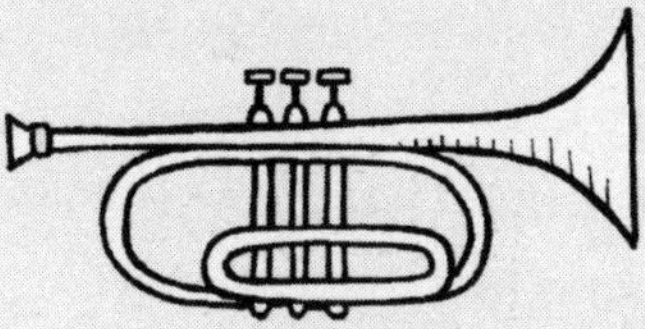

Trumpet
Adds a lot of puff

Kettledrum
Beating heart of the team

Piano
Key part of the team

Viola
A plucky competitor

FORWARDS

Violin
Highly-strung

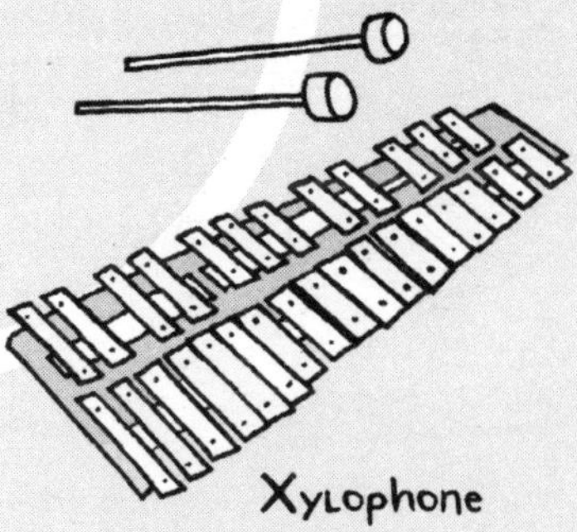

Xylophone
Always hits the woodwork

HANDEL ON THE TROPHY

If you are a football fan, then there's one piece of classical music that is guaranteed to fill you with excitement: the anthem that is played before every Champions League match. It's the one that belts out the line THE CHAMPIONS!

The Champions League anthem is literally a tune fit for a king. Called "Zadok the Priest", it was originally written three hundred years ago by George Handel for the coronation of King George II in 1727, and has been played at the coronation of every single British king and queen since then.

The tune is rousing and grand and exciting – just what is needed for a big event like a coronation or a game of football between Europe's top teams.

The version that is used in the Champions League is a rearrangement of Handel's original, with new words written by Tony Britten, a British writer of radio and TV jingles. It was a tricky job because UEFA asked him to include words in its three official languages: English, French and German. He translated hundreds of words and in the end chose this for his chorus:

The fact that the music chosen is classical, with soaring violins and choir-like voices, adds to the magic of the occasion, turning the stadium into a massive, open-air opera house.

Players love it. Luis Suarez calls the music "incredible", Zinédine Zidane says "it's magic above all else" and it even gives Thiago Silva goosebumps.

Britten likes watching the Champions League on television but doesn't always listen to his anthem before the match. Sometimes he takes the opportunity to go to the loo because he knows exactly how long the song is! Wow-wee!

ELGAR OF HONOUR

English composer Sir Edward Elgar wrote one of the world's first football songs in 1898 after watching his favourite team Wolverhampton Wanderers play Stoke City. He would cycle 64 kilometres to watch Wolves, so he really liked them! The newspaper reports after the game described how Wolves striker Billy Malpass "banged the leather for goal". Elgar loved the phrase so much that he set it to music, composing a short piano piece that was titled "He Banged the Leather for Goal". It was performed for the first time to raise money for a church in Wolverhampton in 2010 – over a century after he first wrote it!

MUSIC QUIZ

1. **What is the name of Antonio Vivaldi's famous series of violin concertos?**

a) Four Seasons
b) Four Trophies
c) Four Cheeses
d) Fork Handles

2. **What instrument does former Czech Republic goalkeeper Petr Čech play in his spare time?**

a) Piano
b) Drums
c) Triangle
d) Guitar

3. **Famous Russian composer Dmitri Shostakovich was a passionate fan of Zenit St Petersburg. He wrote a ballet about a football club that did what?**

a) Wore tutus for away matches
b) Was caught in a match-fixing scandal
c) Lost every game it played
d) Featured a player called Gareth Ballet

4. **Why was it tough for Ludwig van Beethoven to be a composer?**

a) For much of his adult life he was deaf.
b) He never played the piano.
c) He also played football for Germany.
d) He slept in a van.

5. **Former England striker Dion Dublin played the trumpet, but what was his other musical claim to fame?**

a) He was a dancer in an Ariana Grande video.
b) He taught Ed Sheeran to play guitar.
c) He invented a percussive instrument called the Dube.
d) He wrote a song called "Duby Du" which topped the charts.

Tuesday
Lesson 3+4

COMPUTER SCIENCE

This lesson we're going to be looking ahead – way ahead!

We are going to make some predictions about what the world will be like in fifty years' time, when many of you might have children, or even grandchildren, of your own. Forward thinking!

Already we live in a digital world of smartphones, mechanical robots and computer games. We're going to think about how these technologies might develop as computers become faster and more powerful. And we'll also ask, what will this mean for football?

Of course, we cannot be 100 per cent sure what life will be like in 2069. The future will always be unpredictable. But we can make educated guesses based on our experience of digital technology so far. Every year computers get better and better, able to execute commands faster and store more information in their memories. There is no reason to think that the pace of change will slow down. It might even accelerate!

Look out everyone! The future is heading our way!

ENTER THE ROBOTS

Technology: Robot

What is it: A machine that performs a task by itself.

Current state: Robots controlled by computers are used in many areas of modern life. For example, car factories have robots that help build cars, hospitals have tiny robots to help with surgical procedures and armies have robot vehicles that can drive without anyone in them. None of these robots, however, looks like a human.

In the last few years, scientists have also been building human-like robots that move convincingly on two legs and writing programmes for these robots that result in the robot making human-like decisions. These robots are being developed in order to perform certain human tasks, such as assisting the elderly or disabled people, or performing rescue missions in situations like fires where humans would not survive.

Football is currently at the forefront of robot research! That's because one of the biggest competitions in robotics is the RoboCup, the World Cup of robot football, in which teams of robots play football against each other. Every robot taking part must move independently and make decisions independently of the other members of its team. Scientists are so keen for their teams to win the RoboCup that the event is helping push forward robot technology. However, they have a long way to go. The robots still look more like toys than humans, and they struggle to play without falling over. Whoops!

FOOTBALL SCHOOL PREDICTS...

We think that by 2069, scientists will be able to build robots that genuinely look and behave like humans. A robot that is indistinguishable from a person is called an **android**. Androids will be able to do many jobs much better than humans, since they will be built of stronger material than flesh and bones, and will be controlled by computers that can process more information, and at faster speeds, than the human brain.

Androids would be fearsome footballers, since they would easily be able to run at speeds of up to 100 miles an hour, and they would be able to kick a ball so fast you could barely see it. It will be possible to write a programme for an android that gives it such accuracy at shooting that it will never miss, and you could give them 360-degree vision so they know exactly where to pass the ball. An android goalkeeper would have an almost instant reaction time. Electric!

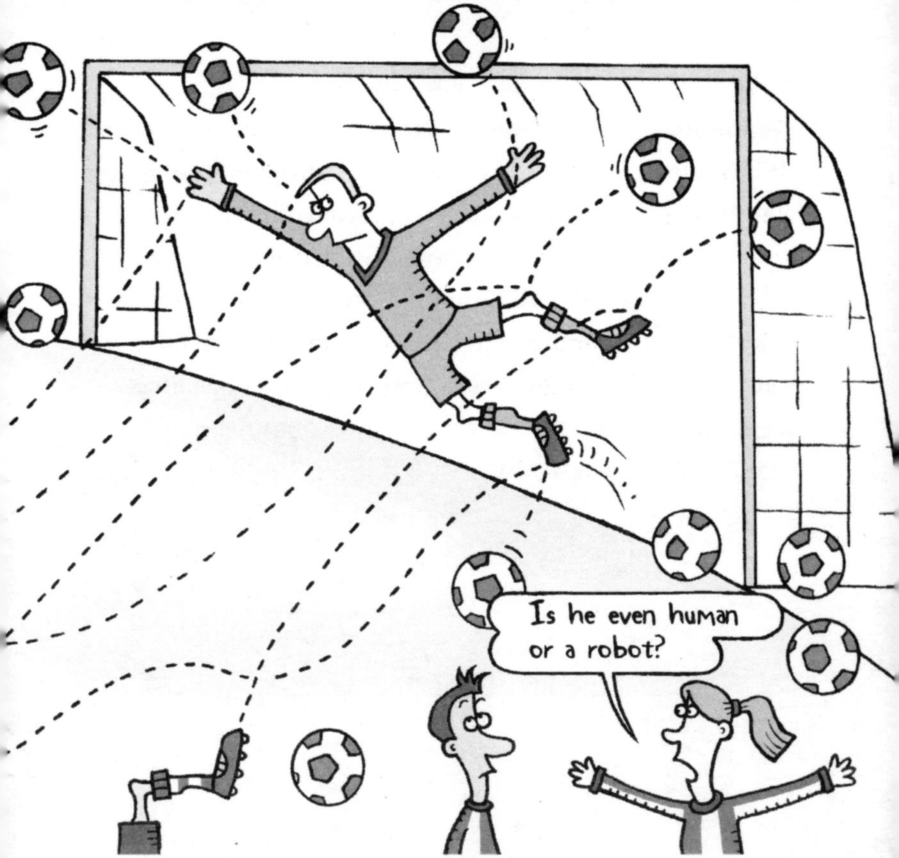

Here are some ways androids may change football:

- **Android Premier League**: teams where every player is an android.
- **Human-android football**: FIFA changes the rules of football to allow every team to field a certain number of androids in their starting line-ups.
- **Personal android**: an android you can practise your dribbling and shooting skills against. The android might have several playing levels, so you could start at the lowest level and gradually increase as you get better and better.

OUT OF THIS WORLD

Technology: Virtual reality (VR)

What is it: A computer simulation in which you put on a headset that makes you feel completely immersed in a three-dimensional digital world. The headset blocks out all outside light, so the wearer can only see what is on the screen inside it. This experience is called virtual reality since the reality that you see around you when wearing the headset is not the real world, but a computer-generated version of the real world.

Current state: VR headsets are already available to buy and software companies have begun releasing games for them. The headsets are used in conjunction with a joystick, which the user needs to control their moves in the game. VR headsets can also be used for watching films and training pilots, doctors and other professionals by immersing them in simulations of their workplaces.

Football is in on the action too! Some clubs get their players to play a special VR game as part of their training. Once the headset is on, the player finds themselves in a football game and must choose which team-mate to pass the ball to. Clubs believe that the game improves skills like decision-making, anticipation, resilience and the ability to scan the space around you.

FOOTBALL SCHOOL PREDICTS...

We predict that in 2069, instead of having to wear a bulky headset and use a joystick in order to experience VR, you will be able to wear VR contact lenses and a **haptic suit**, which is a bodysuit full of sensors. Your movement in the haptic suit will control your behaviour in the computer game. So, for example, if you kick in the haptic suit, you will kick in the game. Eventually, there will be no need for even haptic suits, since the VR sensors will be inserted into your skin and you will hardly notice them. The experience of being in a virtual, computer-generated world will then be almost the same as being in the real world.

Fans wearing VR kit will be able to:

- Have the full experience of watching any football game they like from the best seats, without leaving their bedrooms.
- Play football against computer-generated versions of all their favourite players.

Professional footballers wearing VR kit will be able to:

- Play computer-generated versions of their opponents in order to prepare for matches.
- If a player wears VR kit during a game, it will be possible for fans to experience the game as if they are the player, since everything that the player sees, hears and feels will be transmitted to the VR kit being worn by the fan.

This is edge-of-the-seat stuff!

EE AYE ADD-IO

Technology: Augmented reality (AR)

What is it: The inclusion of digital images in your view of the real world. This technology is called augmented reality because you are augmenting – which means adding to – what you see in the real world.

Current state: AR apps for smartphones already exist. In these apps, the phone displays the camera view but adds digitally-generated images on top, like the lens function on Snapchat, where you can add funny digital shapes to people's faces, or in the game *Pokémon Go*, where you see digital Pokémon creatures that appear to live in the outside world.

AR glasses are glasses that enable the wearer to see digital images added to the real world. One of the apps developed for these glasses enables you to see a football match on a table. The glasses add a digital pitch to the tabletop, with tiny, three-dimensional digital footballers playing on it. Now there's a good reason to tidy up the plates after dinner!

FOOTBALL SCHOOL PREDICTS...

In the future, we think you will be able to get the AR experience by wearing AR contact lenses. It will be possible to see digitally-generated images existing in the real world wherever you look. For example, you could set your AR contact lenses to:

- Display the name, age and birthday of every person you meet. (Only you will see this information, since the images appear inside your contact lenses.) This will be good for Alex who is always forgetting people's names.
- Display all the stats you want about any footballer when you are watching a game of football. This will be good for Ben who always wants to know how many penalties a player has scored.

An AR haptic suit will allow you to fully interact with computer-generated images while staying in the real world. For example, you would be able to play football against a computer-generated footballer in your back garden. In fact, if all your friends wore AR haptic suits, you could play a game in your local park against a team of computer-generated players. One weekend you could play Barcelona, and the next Brazil. Kickabouts will never be the same again!

FABULOUS FABRICS

In 2069, we predict you will be able to buy football shirts where the entire fabric is a digital display. This would allow advertisers to have TV adverts on shirts, and it would mean that the teams could change their shirt colours at any stage during the match. Go Reds! We mean Blues! We mean Greens!

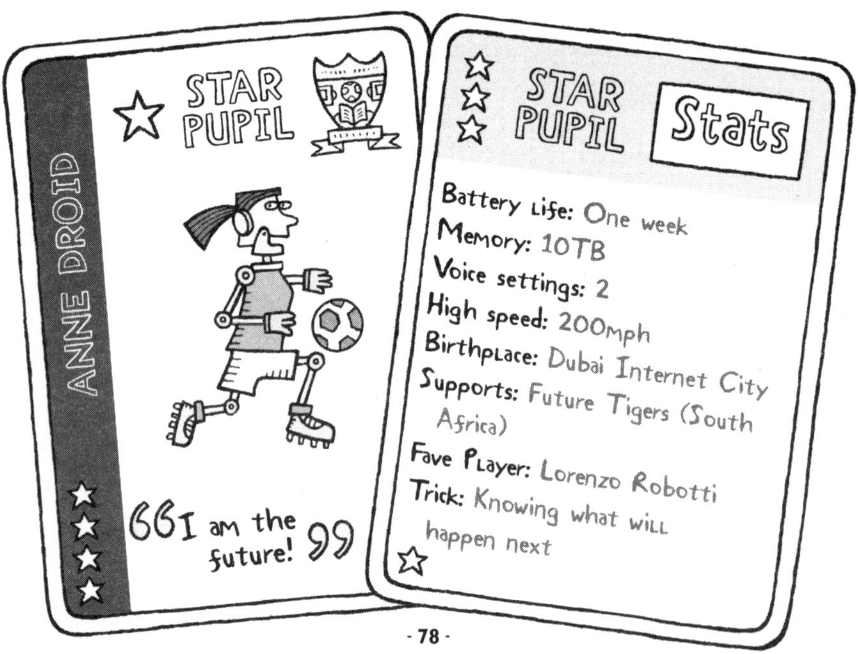

COMPUTER SCIENCE QUIZ

1. **What does VR stand for?**

a) Vegans rule!
b) Virtual reality
c) Very rong
d) Vroom

2. **What does the verb "to augment" mean?**

a) To increase something by adding to it
b) To have an argument
c) To play computer games
d) To be born in August

3. **What type of robot is Wall-E from the film of that name?**

a) A footballer
b) A police officer
c) A traffic warden
d) A rubbish compactor

4. **What is the name given to body clothing with VR sensors?**

a) Hippy suit
b) Happy suit
c) Haptic suit
d) Tiptop suit

5. **What job at some football clubs is already done by a robot? (This robot is a machine with a computer in it but it does not look like a human.)**

a) Washing the players' hair
b) Mowing the pitch
c) Selling programmes
d) Cheering from the stands

Tuesday
Lesson 5

PHILOSOPHY

Hey everyone, this lesson is for losers! For failures, flops, underachievers and also-rans.

Yes, we mean you. Every single one of you.

And us too.

We're all losers. We all mess up from time to time. We all suffer rejections, knock-backs and disappointments. It's part of being human. Sometimes, life sucks!

But failing is important. It is only through our mistakes that we can learn and grow. Losing is not the opposite of winning, it is part of winning.

Every footballer who has ever achieved success has also had their fair share of setbacks. Often, it was these setbacks that pushed them to become stronger.

Philosophy is a subject that asks questions about what we value in life. For example, how do you judge success and how can you best achieve it?

We are all losers, definitely. But we can all be winners too.

IT'S ALL RELATIVE

FIFA maintains a ranking of all 211 national football teams based on their recent performances.

In 2013, Brazil were 22nd and it was a national humiliation.

In 2015, the Faroe Islands were 74th and it was cause for national jubilation.

Why the different reactions? Well, Brazil had spent a decade as the top-ranked team and 22nd was their worst ever position. It was a crisis!

On the other hand, the Faroe Islands – a remote and chilly archipelago in the North Sea with a population of only 50,000 people – had achieved their best ever position. It has been argued that by reaching the giddy heights of 74th place, they became the most successful team by country population in the history of football! Fair old Faroes!

The fabulous feat of the Faroese shows that success is not always about finishing first. In football, only one team can ever win the biggest trophies and often the teams that do are those with the biggest advantages: they are the biggest countries or the clubs with the best players, the best coach, the most money to spend on transfers and wages or, in a knock-out tournament, the easiest draw.

Instead, success means different things to different people. Let's look at the 2018 World Cup as an example. France beat Croatia 4–2 in a dramatic final and won the competition. They were deservedly crowned world champions, but were not the only winners. The following countries all exceeded expectations and consider themselves to have had a "successful" World Cup.

TEAM	WORLD CUP POSITION	SUCCESS
Croatia	Runner-up	Smallest country by population to reach World Cup final
Belgium	Third place	This small country reached semi-final for first time
Russia/Sweden	Quarter-finals	Surprised many to reach final 8
Mexico/Japan	Round of 16	Qualified from tricky group draw
Iceland	Group stage	Smallest country to reach World Cup
Peru	Group stage	First World Cup for 36 years
Panama	Group stage	First World Cup in its history
American Samoa	Qualifiers	First World Cup qualifying victory

France may have lifted the trophy but the 2018 World Cup had so many different winners! What a success!

TUCHEL TIPS

We spoke to coach Thomas Tuchel after the team he used to coach, Borussia Dortmund, had finished second in the German top division. "Points are not the only way to judge my work, so how else can we judge it?" Tuchel asked. We gave him some suggestions, which he liked!

Just as it is up to football teams to define their own measures of success and failure, the same is true in our own lives. We can't all be top of the class in maths or the best in our families at dancing (Ben definitely isn't!). So we need to set ourselves different targets based on what we think is realistic for our own abilities and resources.

Once we have set our target, we need to approach the challenge in the best way.

CASE STUDY

IN THE RIGHT MIND

Alex and Ben decided to start running. They both found it hard. But they reacted in very different ways.

What do you think happened? Alex gave up because he did not think he could improve. He was fixed in his thoughts, telling himself, "I am just not good enough at this and will never get better". This type of attitude is often called a "**fixed mindset**".

But Ben carried on because he wanted to see if he could improve. That motivated him to push himself, although it was hard, and each improvement he made inspired him to get even better. This type of attitude is called a "**growth mindset**".

Scientists have done lots of work comparing fixed mindsets and growth mindsets. Those with a fixed mindset – who think that they cannot improve at something they struggle with – tend to avoid challenges and stick to easy tasks. Because they think that they can't improve, they don't improve.

Those with a growth mindset – who are more comfortable with making mistakes and better at coping with failure – get stuck in! We are not pushing ourselves if we never make mistakes, so don't be afraid to get things wrong or not come up to scratch. If you fail once, try again or try a different way. The effort you put in, or the new strategy you use, will be worth it.

We do learn from our mistakes, so let's embrace them. Even if a new task is difficult, stick with it. Many professional footballers have had to bounce back from failure or adversity to make it in their career.

FOUR TIPS FOR TIP-TOP SUCCESS

1. Set high expectations

Don't just give yourself easy tasks to complete. Setting yourself a tough but realistic challenge will give you additional belief that you can do it – even if it does take time – and that will eventually strengthen your own self-confidence.

2. Don't give up

Lots of things are difficult in life. The brain is constantly absorbing new information and anything that is difficult is growing the brain. Remember: even if you are struggling, you are still learning.

3. Mistakes are fine!

There's nothing wrong with making mistakes as long as we can learn from them. Alex has made some big mistakes with his clothes for a start! If you use each mistake as a learning opportunity, you will improve quicker. Even Alex's jumpers are great now...

4. Having a go is the most important thing

As we have seen, we can't always win. The best thing we can do is focus on the effort we've made or the strategies we have used, and always try our best. We can't control outside factors, but we can control the effort we put in – so let's all try!

THE COMEBACK KIDS

None of the following players were born superstars. They all faced challenges from an early age, learned from their mistakes and worked hard to be where they are now. They are inspiring role models and we can learn from them.

Sam Kerr (Australia)

Kerr almost quit football aged 19 after injuries to her knee and foot left her out of action for almost 18 months. She told her mum that she wanted to give up, but she still kept working hard. After her comeback, she became one of the most feared strikers in world football, breaking goal-scoring records in Australia and the USA, winning the 2017 Asian Women's Footballer of the Year award and being shortlisted for FIFA's 2018 Ballon D'Or award. In-Kerr-edible!

Eric Abidal (France)

The French defender was playing for Barcelona aged 31 when he was diagnosed with a cancerous tumour in his liver. He had an operation to remove the tumour and returned to action just three months later. His first game back was the 2011 Champions League final, which Barcelona won! One year later, he had a liver transplant. He faced not just the end of his career but possibly his life. Yet despite such serious medical problems, he was able to battle back to full health and played for another two years before retiring.

Roberto Baggio (Italy)
The Italy forward was the world's best player when he stepped up to take a penalty in the 1994 World Cup final shoot-out. But he missed the target and Brazil won the trophy. Baggio had nightmares after his historic failure but he continued to take, and score, penalties. His goals helped Juventus (in 1995) and AC Milan (in 1996) win Italy's league title. He showed that even the best players have to deal with failure.

Harry Kane (England)
The England captain and 2018 World Cup Golden Boot winner was rejected by Arsenal when he was eight. He was determined to prove the Gunners wrong but even as a teenager he still faced challenges when he was stuck on the bench at lower-league teams. He vowed to keep working hard and take his chance when it came; he did just that in November 2014, scoring his first Premier League goal for Spurs. He has since scored over 100 top-flight goals and captained England at a World Cup. Arsenal's loss was Spurs's gain!

Lionel Messi (Argentina)
One of the greatest footballers of all time almost never made it. As a youngster, Messi's body did not create enough chemicals to grow properly. He underwent a course of treatment and had to inject himself with a needle every night in one of his legs. Aged 13, he moved to Barcelona, which was the only club willing to pay for the treatment. He lived in Spain with his father, Jorge, leaving his mother and three siblings back in Argentina. Messi had the choice to return home but, despite finding things tough, vowed to stay in Spain and prove himself. We can now say he did a pretty good job!

Fara Williams (England)
The Lionesses' all-time leading appearance-maker fell out with her family as a teenager and was homeless for six years. She lived in hostels and sometimes slept on the street. Williams developed tremendous resilience through adversity and football helped her during this tough period in her life. "Football gave me the focus and belief that I was good at something," she said. She has since repaired relations with her family.

ROCHDALE MINDSET

Rochdale, a small team based in Manchester, holds the record for seasons spent in the bottom division of English professional football's four leagues: 78 in all. Since they joined the Football League in 1921, they have not won a single trophy. But that does not stop Rochdale players from trying – nor the fans from supporting them! Rochdale average over 3,000 fans for every home game, and we salute them all for their patience and support – and the players for still believing!

PHILOSOPHY QUIZ

1. When is it too late to start developing a growth mindset?

a) Aged 12
b) Aged 21
c) Aged 40
d) It's never too late!

2. What word, which means continuing when faced with difficulty, is required for a growth mindset?

a) Assistance
b) Resistance
c) Persistence
d) Subsistence

3. Which team made its first ever appearance at the 2018 World Cup?

a) Peru
b) Panama
c) Japan
d) Sweden

4. Which naturally occurring phenomenon is often used to illustrate growth mindset, showing that a small piece of success comes alongside large amounts of perseverance, sacrifice, mistakes and opportunity?

a) Waterfall
b) Iceberg
c) Puddle
d) Tornado

5. Real Madrid are one of the most successful clubs in the world but what was their biggest defeat?

a) 1–11 to Barcelona
b) 0–6 to Valencia
c) 2–10 to AC Milan
d) 1–8 to Espanyol

Wednesday

SCHOOL TRIP

Wrap up warm! Take some water! Don't forget your jet pack! We're going on a school trip with a difference in this lesson: visiting the most extreme places where football matches have taken place. Our journey around the world will take in the highest, the driest and some of the coldest matches in history.

Football truly is the global game. Its popularity not only stretches to some of these far-out corners of the world, but to the edges of the atmosphere too. Hold on tight!

WHERE IN THE WORLD?

Destination: ANTARCTICA
• The world's coldest, windiest and driest continent
• Most of Antarctica is covered in ice all year round
• Home to 12 million penguins
• Location of the South Pole
ANTARCTICA

EXTREME DESTINATION 1: COLD FEET

Venue: Union Glacier

Location: A glacier in the Antarctic mainland about 1,100km from the South Pole, where during the summer months there is a Chilean research station and the continent's only tourist camp.

Conditions: Summer temperatures are between -25°C and -1°C. The temperature never gets above freezing, ever!

Who lives there? Antarctica has no native residents, but it has a community of scientists who live in research stations. In the winter about 1,000 people are spread out in about 40 permanent stations across the continent. In the summer temporary bases are set up like the ones at Union Glacier, which brings the total number of people in Antarctica to about 5,000.

Who plays football? The people staying at the bases play to keep fit and have fun.

Where do they play? On the ice, with sticks or skis for goalposts. The ice needs to be checked for holes, which could cause injuries.

Famous matches: In 2015, David Beckham flew to the tourist camp on Union Glacier as part of a project to show how football unites everyone in the world. The former England captain played in a match alongside guides, chefs, medics and mechanics who worked at the camp. The same year, the camp's team drove a Caterpillar truck to the Chilean station where they played against a group of Chilean scientists and soldiers. Chilly!

Another match played one hundred years ago is captured in some of the most famous photographs of Antarctica. In 1915, the British explorer Ernest Shackleton was attempting to be the first person to cross Antarctica via the South Pole when his ship, *Endurance*, got stuck in ice. For several months, he and his crew were stranded on a floating sheet of ice. To keep everyone motivated, Shackleton encouraged the men to play football. They used oars for goalposts and flattened the ice so the ball would move smoothly across it. Photographs from the trip show the crew playing football fully clothed, as penguins and seals looked on. One crew member fell through the ice and into the freezing water. That's what we call a cold snap! It took Shackleton a further fourteen months to guide his crew to the safety of dry land, in what is considered to be one of the most epic survival stories of all time. Captain fantastic!

WHERE IN THE WORLD?

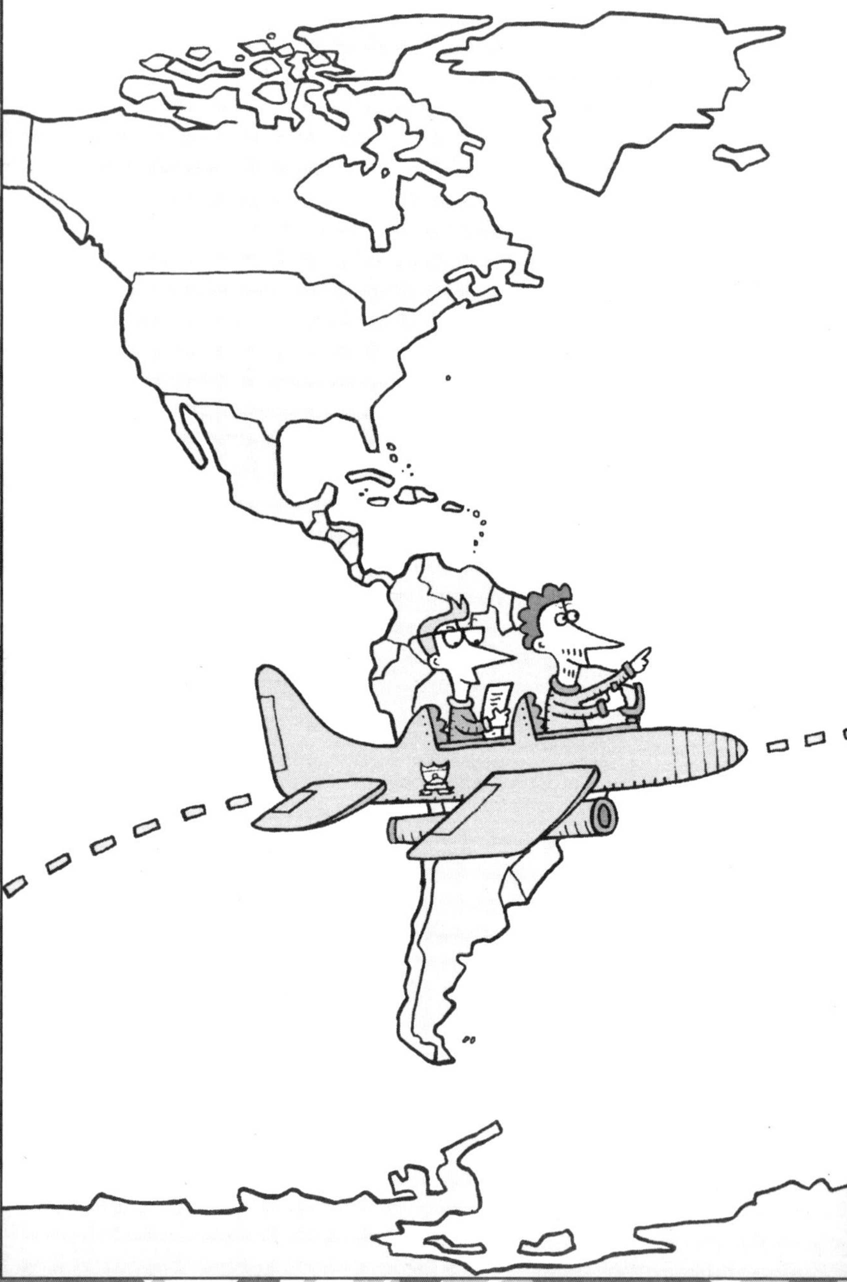

Destination: MOUNT KILIMANJARO
• Highest mountain in Africa
• Dormant volcano
• Home to the Kilimanjaro two-horned chameleon and the Kilimanjaro shrew
AFRICA
MOUNT KILIMANJARO
Tanzania

EXTREME DESTINATION 2: HITTING THE HEIGHTS

Venue: Mount Kilimanjaro

Location: Tanzania

Conditions: The summit of Kilimanjaro is 5,895m above sea level. At such a high altitude the air has only about half the amount of oxygen as it has at sea level, which means it is much harder to fill your lungs with the oxygen you need to breathe. As a result, people who climb that high can suffer from altitude sickness, which gives you headaches and makes you feel nauseous.

Who lives there? At the top of Kilimanjaro, no one!

Who plays football? In 2017, two women's teams took part

in the highest-altitude football game ever played. The pitch was in a volcanic crater only 100m below Kilimanjaro's summit. The two squads took six days to climb up the mountain, before they marked out a full-sized pitch on a bed of ash. The game was organized by Equal Playing Field, a movement dedicated to inspiring women to play football. One player, Haneen Al-Khateeb, was proud to have played at such a height. "I did it for every girl and woman who didn't get the opportunity to be who she might be," she said. "I did it because women footballers deserve to be seen and respected." Two players were substituted off with shortness of breath and the final score was 0–0. What a long way to go for a goalless draw!

WHERE IN THE WORLD?

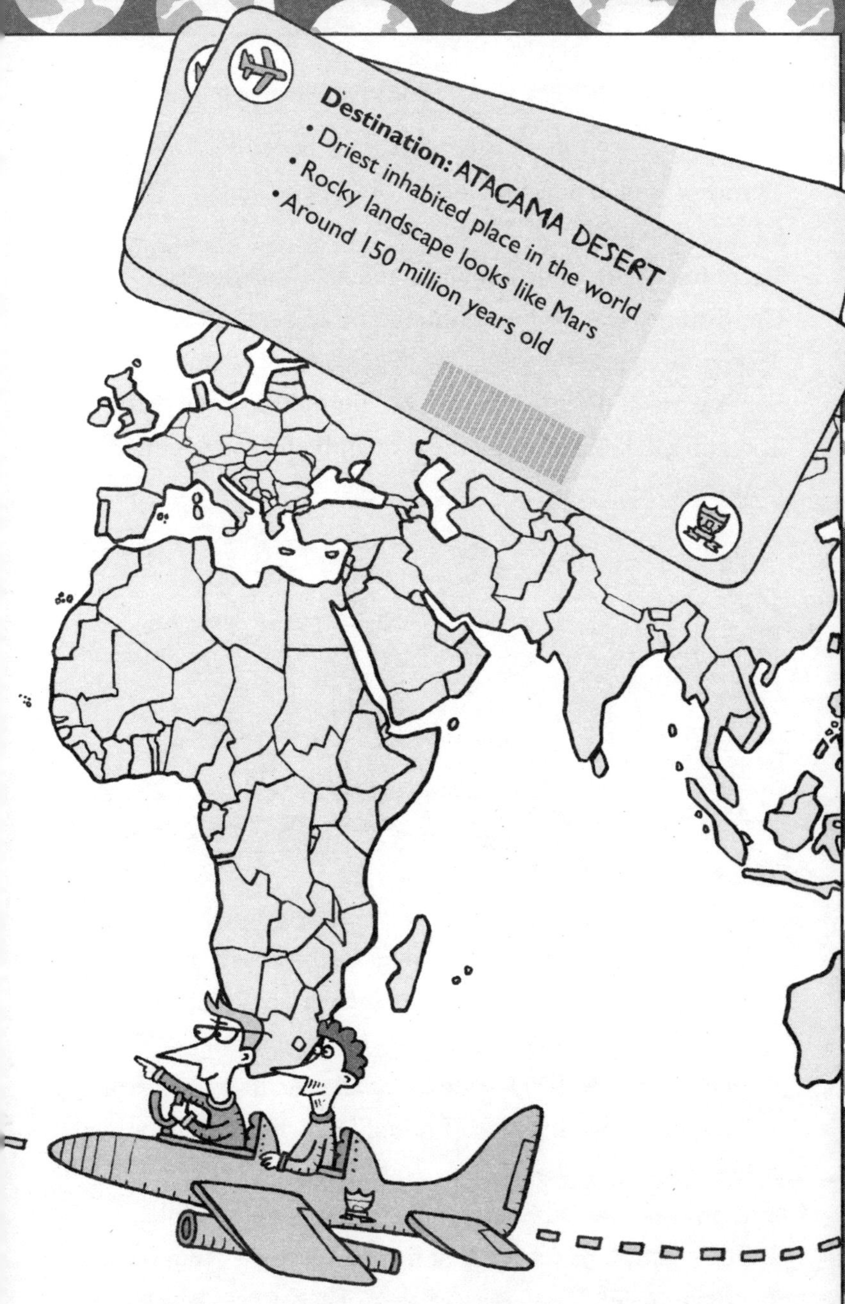

Destination: ATACAMA DESERT
• Driest inhabited place in the world
• Rocky landscape looks like Mars
• Around 150 million years old

EXTREME DESTINATION 3: DRY AND DRY AGAIN

Venue: El Cobre Stadium, home of Chilean club CD Cobresal

Location: El Salvador, a town in the Atacama desert

Conditions: The average annual rainfall here is just 15mm. (Compare that to London, which has almost 600mm.) Some parts of the Atacama are not thought to have had any rainfall at all between the sixteenth and the twentieth centuries.

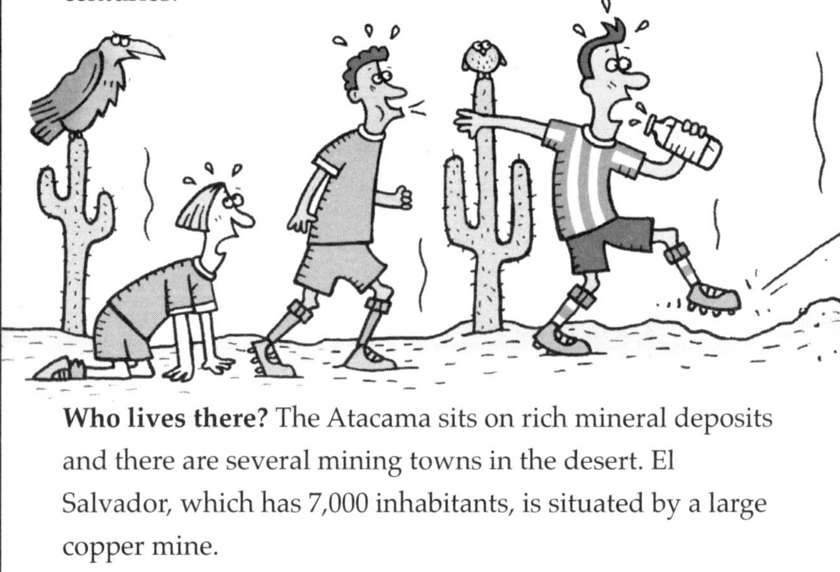

Who lives there? The Atacama sits on rich mineral deposits and there are several mining towns in the desert. El Salvador, which has 7,000 inhabitants, is situated by a large copper mine.

Who plays football? Despite its small size, its remoteness and its world-beating lack of rain, El Salvador has a football club that plays in the Chilean first division. CD Cobresal were founded in 1979 and, in 2015, they became Chilean league champions for the first time, winning a dramatic game on the final day of the season. The success became known as The Miracle of Cobresal.

The grass pitch at El Cobre needs to be watered constantly because the air is so arid and there is almost never a chance of rain. When the stadium was built, the turf was brought in from more than 100 miles away.

Famous players: Iván Zamorano, who played for Real Madrid and Inter Milan and is regarded as one of Chile's best ever players, started at Cobresal. Another former player, Franklin Lobos, became a miner after retiring. In 2010, he became known around the world when he and 32 other miners were trapped for 69 days down a copper mine in the Atacama. The mine collapsed when the men were 700m underground. Amazingly, the miners were kept alive by supplies passed through tubes underground and were sent notes by their loved ones urging them to stay positive. A fortnight after they were eventually rescued, the miners played a football match against their rescuers – and the president of Chile – at the national stadium.

WHERE IN THE WORLD?

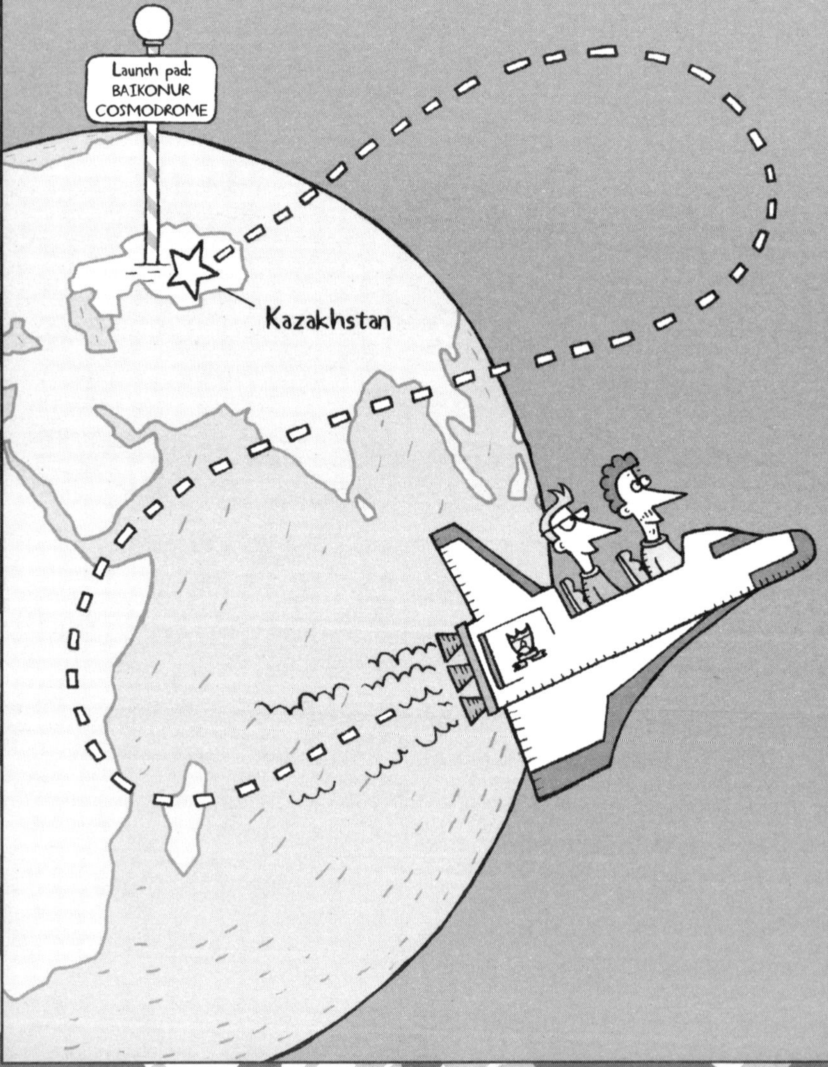

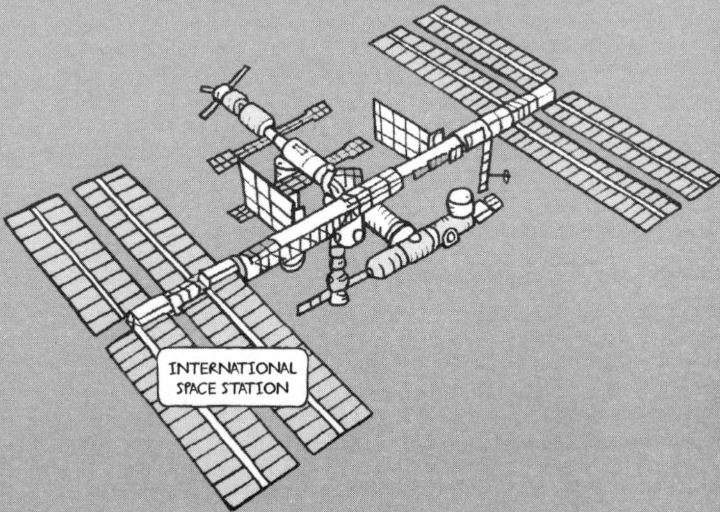

Destination: INTERNATIONAL SPACE STATION

- Aluminium spaceship 73m high and 109m wide
- About 250 miles above Earth
- Orbits the Earth at 17,100 miles an hour
- Has been continually occupied since 2000

EXTREME DESTINATION 4: REACHING FOR THE STARS

Venue: International Space Station (ISS)

Location: At the edge of the Earth's atmosphere, about 250 miles high in the sky. The ISS is constantly moving and takes roughly 90 minutes to orbit the Earth.

Conditions: A lack of **gravity** means that items do not fall when you drop them and if you push something it will float through the air. Even though the temperature outside of the station varies from –157°C to 121°C, a thermal control system inside keeps the temperature comfortable for humans.

Who lives there? The ISS usually houses six astronauts at any one time.

Who plays football? In 2018, an official FIFA ball was taken up to the station, where Russian astronauts Anton Shkaplerov and Oleg Artemyev played an informal game with each other inside one of the ISS laboratory units. They made amazing acrobatic kicks as they floated in the air. But they didn't kick the ball too hard in case they broke something! Shkaplerov brought the ball back to Earth, where it was a feature of the 2018 World Cup opening ceremony in Moscow. A young boy kicked the ball to the World Cup mascot Zabivaka, in what was the first kick of the tournament.

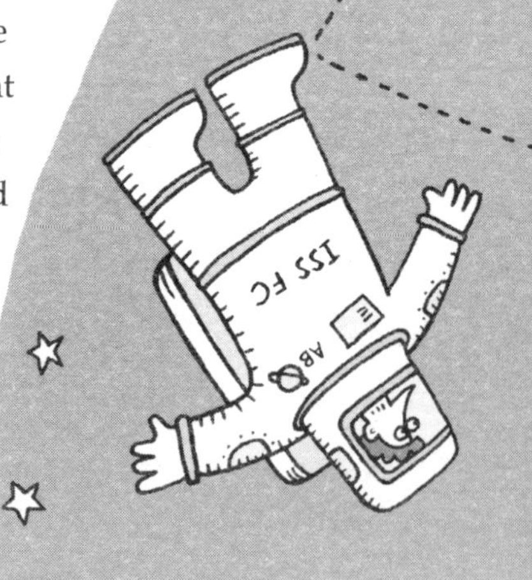

ISS
SG
ISS FC
DJ
ISS FC
BL
ISS FC

FISHING FOR GOALS

The winger floats in a cross only for the striker to dive in the area … welcome to the crazy world of underwater football. A two-a-side game took place in a huge fish-filled aquarium in north-east China in 2014. The players wore oxygen tanks and goggles, and used a ball partially filled with water to create buoyancy so that it didn't float to the surface. Other underwater sports include hockey, rugby and even wrestling, which is known as aquathlon. Deep stuff!

SCHOOL TRIP QUIZ

1. **Which is the world's windiest continent?**

a) Africa
b) Antarctica
c) Asia
d) Australasia

2. **Which of these European capitals has the highest altitude?**

a) Berlin, Germany
b) Bern, Switzerland
c) Madrid, Spain
d) Vienna, Austria

3. **One of the world's most powerful telescopes, which consists of 66 smaller telescopes arranged in a pattern, is called ALMA. What does ALMA stand for?**

a) Amazingly Luminous Mars Action
b) Atacama Large Millimeter Array
c) Arcturus Lunar Made in Atacama
d) Atacama Loves Mega Asteroids

4. **What was the name of the World Cup ball that went to space?**

a) Telsun 18
b) Telmoon 18
c) Telmars 18
d) Telstar 18

5. **What does the Spanish word *cobre*, which gives its name to CD Cobresal's stadium, mean?**

a) Cobra
b) Corn on the cob
c) Copper
d) It's Very Dry Round Here

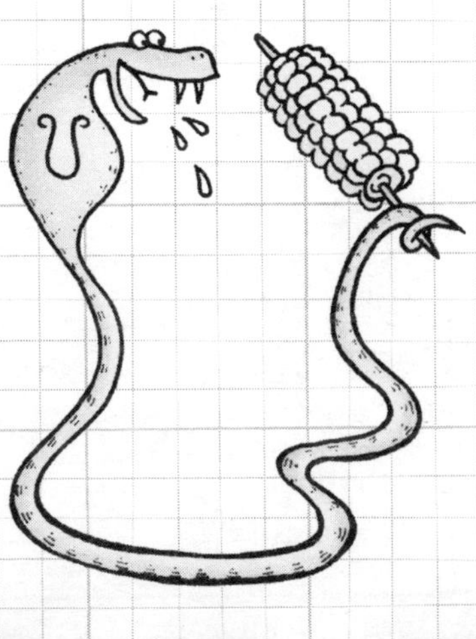

Thursday
Lesson 1+2

HISTORY

If there is something you really want in life, the first step is to work out how to get it.

Let's say you want to watch football on TV but your parents want you to do your homework. You need a plan!

One strategy would be to have a temper tantrum and hope your parents cave in to your demand. This is high risk because they could send you straight to bed.

Another strategy would be flattery. Tell your parents how much you love them. They might be so touched by your words that they decide it would be a nice gesture to let you watch the game. They may fall for this one!

Or you could just do the homework as fast as possible, risk missing the beginning but catch the second half.

In football it's just the same: teams need a gameplan. Attack from the start, or sit deep and score on the break? Long ball or passing game? A coach will choose the system they think will ensure the best result based on the strengths of their players and their knowledge of the opposition. This lesson is about the history of football tactics. In position, everyone!

NUMBERS GAME

Clipboards out!

It's footballing convention to describe team formations with numbers separated by hyphens. There are ten outfield players, so the numbers always add up to ten. Goalkeepers are never forgotten even if they are not mentioned.

When describing a formation, you go through each part of the pitch starting in defence, then moving to midfield and attack. So a 3-5-2 formation will have three defenders, five midfielders and two strikers. In some cases, players will be between areas of the pitch, so a 4-2-3-1 will have four defenders, two defensive midfielders, three attacking midfielders and one striker.

One common truth that runs through the history of tactics is the desire of every coach to find the right balance between attack and defence.

It is often said that attack is the best form of defence. But is defence the best form of attack? Don't sit on de-fence!

Let's look at some of the most famous formations in the history of football.

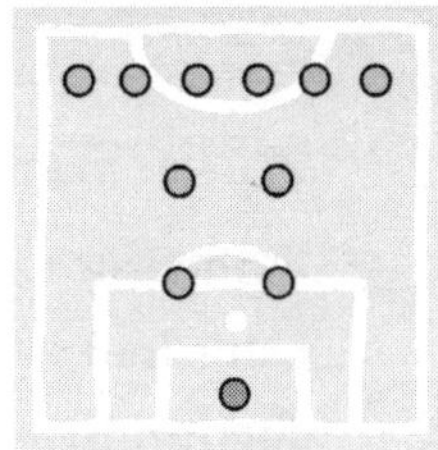

FIRST PASS

Formation: 2-2-6

Decade: 1870s

Tactical breakdown: Passing the ball to team-mates improves results.

History: In football's early years there were no real tactics. If a player had the ball they would just dribble for as long as they could before they lost it. But then the Scots had a brilliant idea: why don't we pass the ball? No one had thought of this before! All of a sudden the players were working as a team – and with six strikers there were plenty of passes to go round. Scotland played this way in the first ever international match in 1872, where they managed to draw 0–0. Soon teams in England were also playing the passing game.

Legacy to football: Teams across Europe copy the idea. Pass!

Importance to the game: 8/10

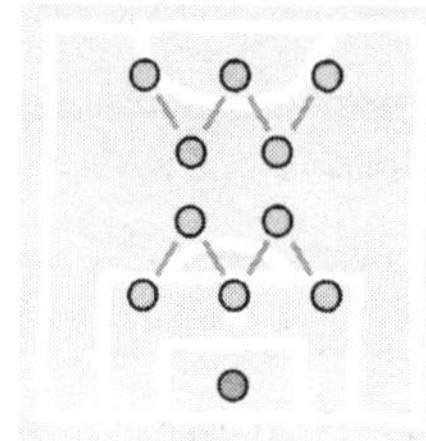

WILY MARKING

Formation: 3-2-2-3
Decade: 1930s
Tactical breakdown: Also known as W-M, this formation positions four midfielders in two lines, so it looks like the letters W and M.
History: W-M was a revolution in football because it was one of the first formations to have players spread evenly throughout the entirety of the pitch. This meant that players had to pass the ball across larger distances. Invented by Arsenal coach Herbert Chapman, W-M was so successful that the Gunners won five league titles in the 1930s and soon it was used by all the English clubs and the national team. W-M! Wonderful Moments! Wise Managers!
Legacy to football: The England national team adopts the W-M formation.
Importance to the game: 7/10

Herbert Chapman was a successful coach at Huddersfield and Arsenal. He came up with some revolutionary ideas that still work today.

SPACE: THE FINAL FRONTIER

Formation: 4-2-4
Decade: 1950s
Tactical breakdown: An extra defender to make it four at the back and more bodies in attack.
History: Tactics are not just about where to put your players – it's also about where not to put them. In the 1950s a formation developed that had lots of space in the middle of the field. It created an exciting game, as players were more able to run into space rather than directly confront opponents. Hungary and Brazil played like this and it inspired teams around the world to play with four defenders.
Legacy to football: Two central defenders became the norm. England, playing with four defenders, wins the 1966 World Cup.
Importance to the game: 9/10

DOOR STOPPER

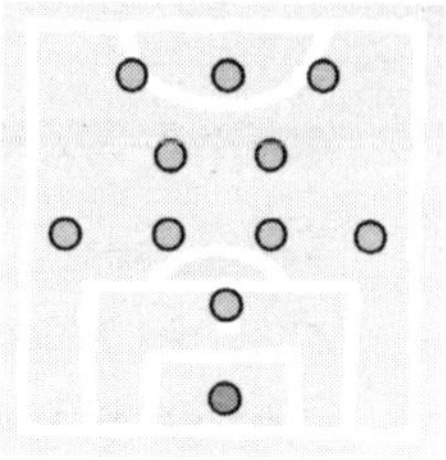

Formation: 1-4-2-3

Decade: 1960s

Tactical breakdown: An ultra-defensive system with an extra player behind the four-man defence.

History: Helenio Herrera, an Argentine coach in charge of Italian side Inter Milan, devised a formation called *catenaccio*, meaning "door lock", since it aimed to keep the goal shut off from opposing strikers. It introduced the idea of the *libero*, or "sweeper", an extra man behind the back four who sweeps up the ball if it comes to him. This system created games with very few goals, and this was one reason the scoring rules were changed to three points (rather than two) for a win to encourage teams to play less defensively.

Legacy to football: More shots from distance to avoid man-marking. Attacking teams rewarded with three points for a win.

Importance to the game: 8/10

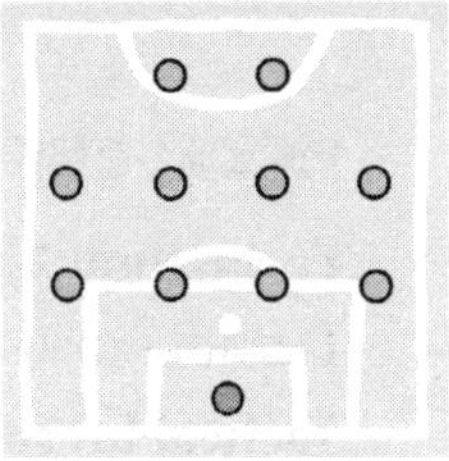

MADE IN ENGLAND

Formation: 4-4-2

Decade: 1970s

Tactical breakdown: A formation with a back-line of defenders, a four-person midfield and a pair of strikers.

History: This was successful when English coaches like Roy Hodgson took charge of Swedish clubs in the 1970s; AC Milan won back-to-back European Cup finals with 4-4-2 in the 1980s; and it dominated the early years of the Premier League in the 1990s. The formation was seen as a sensible way to cover space all over the pitch, with four defenders covering the width of the back-line, a midfield busy with players helping in attack and defence, and two strikers, with whoever receives the ball having someone in close support at all times.

Legacy to football: The strike partnership is born with two forwards operating close to each other. The formation takes off in Italy and England.

Importance to the game: 9/10

MESSI BUSINESS

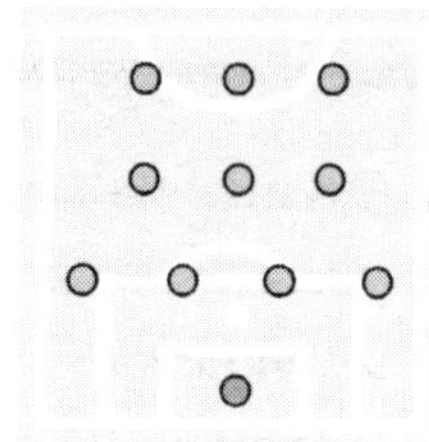

Formation: 4-3-3

Decade: 2000s

Tactical breakdown: Keeping possession and speedy attacks.

History: At Barcelona in the 2000s a new style of football emerged called *tiki-taka*, in which players aimed to keep possession as much as possible through making short and fast passes. Players would often overload on one side of the pitch and then quickly switch it to the other side. Barcelona coach Pep Guardiola would tell his players: "Take the ball, pass the ball." This formation relied on technique and speed of thought rather than height and strength, so shorter players like Lionel Messi, Xavi Hernández and Andrés Iniesta excelled.

Legacy to football: Technique and speed overtakes strength and height as key skills, allowing new players with these skills to succeed.

Importance to the game: 9/10

FORMATIONS OF THE FUTURE

Over the last few pages we've seen seven famous tactical formations. Dozens more have been used over the last hundred years and every year coaches come up with new ones. Tactics are always evolving because whenever one system becomes dominant, coaches devise new strategies to counter that system, which leads to these new strategies becoming dominant, and then more new strategies are again needed.

Coaches need to innovate constantly in order to be one step ahead. Today, coaches love their teams to press high up the pitch, which means their attackers try to win the ball back as close as possible to the opposition goal. They also love versatile players who are smart enough to fill different positions on the pitch – like fullbacks who can play as wingers. In the future, we might see new trends: goalkeepers regularly starting attacks from outside their own area, and more goals from fewer shots as teams become more selective about shooting from distance.

BEYOND THE PAIL

Marcelo Bielsa is one of the most innovative coaches in football. Pep Guardiola and Mauricio Pochettino consider the Argentine, who has coached Chile, Athletic Bilbao, Marseille and Leeds United, a tactical genius. Bielsa's preferred system is a 3-3-1-3. As he likes to watch games pitchside at a low height, at Leeds he sat on an upturned blue bucket, which became a popular item in the club shop. At Marseille, he sat on a cool box, but once got a shock – and a burnt bottom – when someone left a cup of hot coffee there and he sat on it. Ouch!

HISTORY QUIZ

1. What does the Italian term *catenaccio* mean?

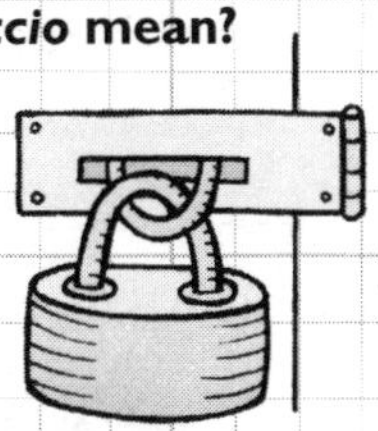

a) Door lock
b) Female cat
c) Garlic bread
d) Offside

2. Which football innovation did Herbert Chapman come up with?

a) Crossbars on goals
b) Penalty shoot-outs
c) Gloves for goalkeepers
d) Assistant referees

3. What is gegenpressing, a strategy used by many modern teams?

a) Wearing nicely ironed kits
b) Players speak only in German to confuse opposition
c) Winning the ball back as soon as it has been lost
d) Goalkeeper and striker switch positions at half-time

4. What new role was named for the position Lionel Messi played for most of his successful career at Barcelona?

a) Big eight
b) False nine
c) Wrong ten
d) Cunning eleven

5. What is a Christmas tree formation?

a) One with no defenders so it's a gift for opponents
b) A 4-3-2-1 which, when written on a sheet, looks like a Christmas tree
c) Any formation used in games played in December
d) A flexible formation for teams who have a player sent off, invented by a Scottish coach called Colin Christmas

Thursday
Lesson 3+4

PSHE

At Football School we love birthdays. Cake! Parties! Presents! But for ancient Alex and grizzled Ben, our birthdays are also a reminder that our dreams of one day playing for England are further and further away.

In this lesson we will be looking at age and how it is relevant to a footballer's performance on the pitch. Do players get better or worse as they get older? When do they reach their peak? We'll be looking at what happens to our bodies in our mature years, and we'll discover that we are living for longer than ever before. This means we can enjoy playing and watching football for longer. Maybe in the future we'll all be sitting down to watch the match with our great-great-great-grandchildren! That would be great, great, great!

But first we're going to take a trip to Japan to meet the world's oldest player.

'Ere we Tokyo!

OLD KING KAZU

With greying hair and wrinkles on his forehead, striker Kazuyoshi Miura scored a goal in the Japanese second division in 2017 that put him in the record books.

Aged 50, the Yokohama FC player became the oldest person to score in the history of professional football. His goal was an incredible achievement, not only for himself but also for humankind, showing that with motivation, preparation and luck, it is possible to keep on playing for longer and longer.

Miura has been a professional footballer for 33 years – incredible considering that in the UK the career of a professional footballer is on average only eight years. In Japan he is a legend. He was one of his country's first football superstars when Japan started a professional league, called the J-League. It was back in 1993 and Miura was both top scorer and winner of the player of the year award. That's so long ago even Ben can barely remember it!

Miura was flamboyant on and off the pitch. He was famous for his trademark goal celebration, a hip wiggle nicknamed the Miura dance. At the end of season awards he wore a snazzy bright red suit, when everyone else wore black.

Known to his fans as "King Kazu", Miura was the first Japanese footballer ever to play in Italy's Serie A, for Genoa, and he also spent time at clubs in Brazil, Croatia and Australia. When he signed for Yokohama aged 38, it was assumed that he was not far off retirement – but he has carried on for more than a decade.

As he has got older he has made fewer appearances. He played 31 times in 2011 aged 44, but since then has never played more than 20 games a season. Still, he occasionally hits the back of the net – and gives his adoring fans another rendition of the Miura dance.

ELIXIR OF YOUTH

So why has Miura been able to play as a professional for so long? He was born with a remarkable physique that has enabled him to maintain a level of fitness well beyond the average for his age and has been lucky not to suffer a career-ending injury. He is also seriously motivated, with a strict daily routine:

Miura's dedication and professionalism have won praise from his coaches and team-mates. King Kazu seems to have the secret to eternal life – maybe he will still be playing when he reaches 100!

GOLDEN OLDIES

Age doesn't have to be a barrier to competing at the highest level. Here are some World Cup record-breakers who led by experience:

NAME	COUNTRY	AGE	OLDEST TO ...	TOURNAMENT
Essam El-Hadary	Egypt	45 years, 161 days	Start a game	2018
Roger Milla	Cameroon	42 years, 39 days	Score a goal	1994
Dino Zoff	Italy	40 years, 133 days	Start the final	1982
Nils Liedholm	Sweden	35 years, 264 days	Score in the final	1958
Cristiano Ronaldo	Portugal	33 years, 130 days	Score a hat-trick	2018

SUPER-STAN

Before Miura, the record for oldest goal-scorer belonged to England's Sir Stanley Matthews, who was 49 years old when he scored his final goal for Stoke City in 1964. Matthews remains the only player to have been knighted – named a Sir – while still an active player. He played in Malta up to the age of 55. Stan-tastic!

SHODDY BODIES

A player as old as Miura is the exception. If you play professionally, you are much more likely to be a teenager than a fifty-something. Many players debut at school age, like Georgia Stanway (16 for Manchester City debut) and Raheem Sterling (17 for Liverpool debut). When you are young, every year you get a little bit bigger, faster and stronger than you were the year before. At some stage you will reach your physical peak – usually around your 30s – and then your athletic performance normally starts to decline. This drop in performance is why most footballers who are still playing at that age start to be overshadowed by their younger team-mates.

Here are three ways that the body changes once you are in your 30s:

HEART

The heart begins to beat a little more slowly, like a battery losing its charge.
Effect: We can't work as hard.

MUSCLES

Our cells are always being destroyed and rebuilt. But as we get older, the breakdown of the cells happens more quickly than their rebuilding, so our muscles get smaller.
Effect: With smaller muscles, we are less strong.

FAT

Our metabolic rate, the rate at which our bodies convert food into energy, lowers as we get older. As a result, we pile on the pounds.
Effect: Less energy to run around the pitch.

BONES

Your bones tend to become thinner, although exercise and eating food high in calcium can help minimize this.
Effect: Reduces bone strength and increases risk of fracture.

It's important to remember that everyone is unique and our bodies all behave differently as we grow older. Our genes, gender, medical history, physical activity level, hormones and diet all play a part. There is no right or wrong to the ageing process – and we can't all live like Miura. For a start, Ben hates ice baths!

AN OLDIE BUT A GOLDIE

Younger players may be faster and more energetic than older ones, but sometimes it is an advantage to be the senior person in the team.

Many good things come with age, such as experience, wisdom and happiness. Just ask your parents!

Former Arsenal coach Arsene Wenger was not so convinced. He believed that players were on a downslope by the age of 30 and refused to hand out contracts longer than one year to any player who had hit 30 – although he admitted it depended on the player's position.

In football, players may get slower with time but they develop other skills, like positional sense and game intelligence, as they have more games under their belt. Often the wisdom and guile of an experienced player can overwhelm the speed and strength of a younger one.

In fact, strikers are on average the youngest players on the pitch – they need energy and speed to run at the goal – while goalkeepers are on average the oldest, since for them experience is often more important than athleticism.

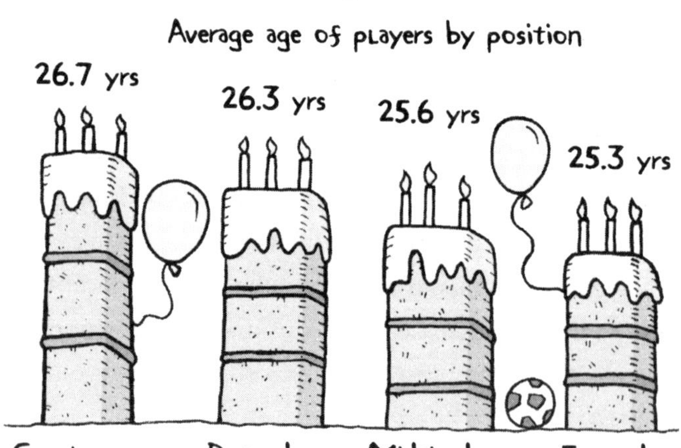

Some players can even overcome their ageing bodies by switching position to extend their careers: when Argentine central midfielder Javier Mascherano was no longer able to cover the pitch as he used to, he moved to centre-back, where his ability to read the game was a valuable skill.

One study looked at the age that players reach their best. It showed that goalkeepers shine later in life. In that position, communication and organization are important skills which improve with age. Goalkeepers peak at age 29, compared to forwards at 27 and midfielders at 25.

LIVE FOR EVER

It's not just that footballers are playing for longer and longer. Humans as a species are living longer too. Life expectancy has risen by seven years over the last few decades – mainly thanks to better healthcare and medical advances in treating diseases. If it continues to grow at the same rate, within a few decades children will expect to live to 100 on average! That's a lot of candles to blow out!

LONG LIFERS

Want to know the secret to a long life? Scientists have focused their research on the countries below, as they are where people live the longest. *Sayonara!*

RANK	COUNTRY	LIFE EXPECTANCY
1	Japan	84.1
2	Switzerland	83.7
3	Spain	83.4
4	Italy	83.3
5	Luxembourg	82.8
22	United Kingdom	81.2

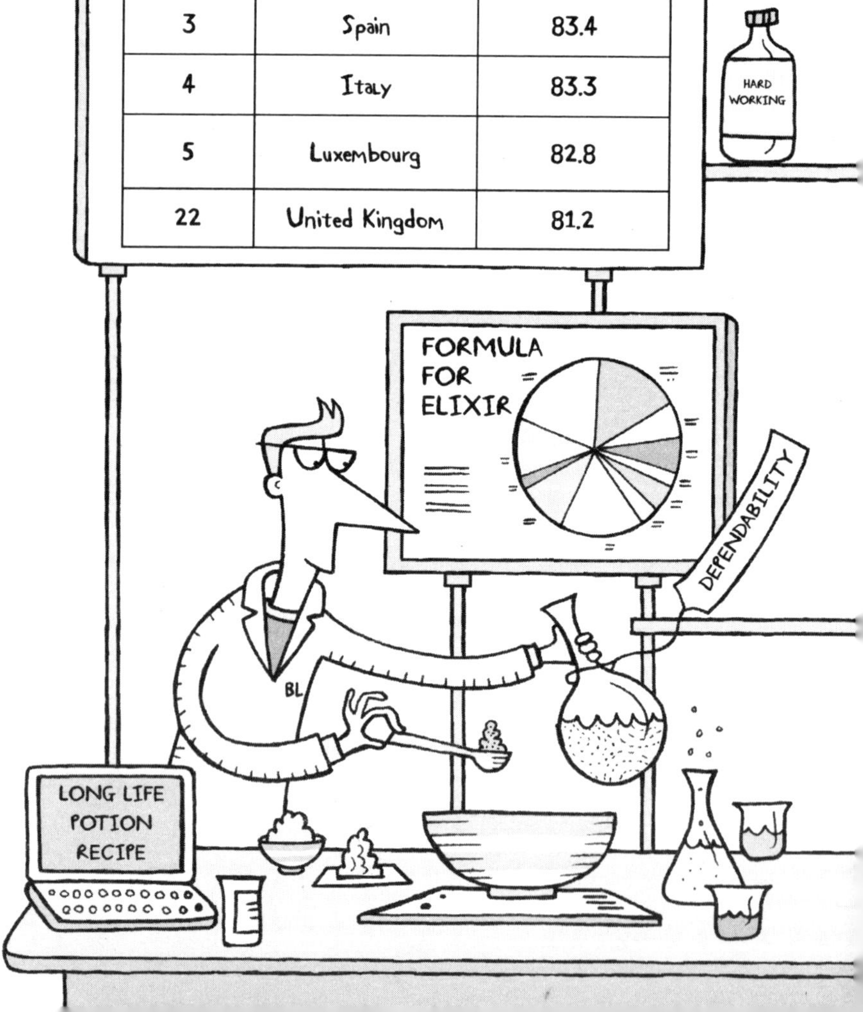

A healthy diet and strong genetic make-up are key ingredients to living a long life. Scientists have claimed that the one personality trait that unites people who live the longest is that they are conscientious; they are dependable and hard-working and don't take risks that might harm themselves. Good news for Alex, who drives very slowly! Other predictors of long life include helping others, staying physically active and hanging out with healthy people!

EURO SO OLD! EURO SO YOUNG!

The average age in Europe's leagues varies quite widely. Smaller nations tend to have younger teams since they are made of home-grown talent, who then get sold to bigger leagues where the average age is higher.

YOUNGEST PLAYERS

COUNTRY	AVERAGE AGE
Croatia	24.2
Slovenia	24.4
Holland	24.6
Serbia	24.9
Slovakia	25

OLDEST PLAYERS

COUNTRY	AVERAGE AGE
Cyprus	27.5
Italy	27.1
Turkey	27
England	26.8
Germany	26.7

PSHE QUIZ

1. **In what position on the pitch are you most likely to improve as you get older?**

a) Goalkeeper
b) Defender
c) Midfielder
d) Striker

2. **Jeanne Calment lived until she was 122 years old and remains the only known person to have lived beyond 120. Where was she from?**

a) Japan
b) Switzerland
c) Germany
d) France

3. **Egypt's Essam El-Hadary became the oldest player to captain a World Cup team but what other record did he break at the 2018 World Cup?**

a) Oldest player to save a World Cup penalty
b) Oldest player to be sent off
c) First player to fall asleep during a match
d) Player with the longest beard

4. **How many goals did Stanley Matthews score in Blackpool's 4–3 1953 FA Cup final win over Bolton that became known as the Matthews final?**

a) 0
b) 1
c) 2
d) 3

5. **When some people grow older, their hair goes grey. This is because the cells in hair follicles, the tissue at the root of each hair strand, create less of which chemical that gives our hair its colour?**

a) Melanin
b) Melanout
c) Popitin
d) Popitout

Thursday
Lesson 5

ENGLISH

We all know the names of our favourite football clubs, but do you know where these names come from? Every name tells a story and in this lesson we're going to look at how British football teams got their names. Are we UNITED in our plan to discover the meaning of each CITY and TOWN? Get ready to discover the club that celebrates Snot, the club named after a prison and the club with a boar in its name. Snort, snort!

British place names reveal the country's ancient history and the names given to football clubs often relate to interesting facts about their origins. You will never read the league table in the same way again.

In the name of Football School, read on!

UNITED WE STAND

Alex United! Ben Rovers!

Put the word "united" or "rovers" after a name and already it sounds like a football club. But who decided to use these words to describe clubs and why?

The word "united" was first used in sports in Sheffield in 1854, when several local cricket clubs decided to merge into one. The new club called themselves the Sheffield United Cricket Club, because the smaller clubs had united to form a bigger one. Howzat!

It took another three decades for football to get in on the action. In 1889, the cricket club decided to field a football team which was also called Sheffield United. This made the Blades the first United in football. Sharp!

A few years later, Newcastle East End and Newcastle West End (the two big football teams in that city) merged. To reflect their joint heritage, they decided on the name Newcastle United. The U-word was catching on.

Then in 1902, a local Manchester team called Newton Heath decided to change their name so as to sound more impressive. They debated calling themselves Manchester Central or Manchester Celtic but in the end chose Manchester United because it sounded grand and inclusive. Since then the word "united" has become so associated with football that it has spread to other countries too.

I WANDERED LONELY AS A CLUB

Rover is a traditional name for a dog. Woof, woof!

Rover is also a word for someone who wanders about with no fixed destination. For this reason, in the nineteenth century, cricket, football and rugby clubs that didn't have permanent home grounds sometimes called themselves Rovers or Wanderers. They roved and wandered around the area playing games wherever they could. Rover is also an old word for pirate, so it made the clubs sound fearsome in their desire for silverware and glory. Clubs called Wanderers were often travelling teams who played just for pleasure. Today the current crop of Rovers (Blackburn, Bristol, Doncaster, Tranmere and Forest Green) and Wanderers (Wolverhampton, Wycombe and Bolton) all have their own stadiums. Wander-ful!

CHALK TALK

One common name in football is as old as Britain itself. The word "Albion" is the oldest known name for the island of Great Britain. It comes from the word *albus,* meaning "white", because the first thing you see when you arrive by boat from the continent is the bright white chalk cliffs of Dover. Albion is still a poetic way to refer to the country, and its name is used by many pubs, streets and sports clubs. The town of West Bromwich used to have a neighbourhood called Albion, which is why the local club is called West Bromwich Albion. Other Albions include Brighton and Hove, Burton and Stirling. Enough information? Ok! Al-bi-on my way!

THERE'S ONLY ONE...

Some clubs have completely unique sports names. There's only one Tottenham Hotspur, Sheffield Wednesday, Leyton Orient and Crewe Alexandra.

For Tottenham, it's a horsey tale. The club was named after the medieval soldier Henry Percy, whose nickname was Hotspur. A spur is a piece of metal that riders wear on their heels to make their horse go faster.

Percy lived 500 years before football was even invented. He got his nickname because, being so fearless on his horse, his spur got hot from being used so often. The descendants of Percy's family owned land near Tottenham in North London, so when local schoolboys wanted a name for their cricket and football club, they decided to honour the famous soldier. However, "hotspur" is also used to describe someone who acts quickly, without thinking about the consequences. Not even Tottenham wants a hotspur in their team!

Sheffield Wednesday got their name because they were originally a cricket club who played their matches on Wednesdays.

Leyton Orient got their name from the Orient Shipping Company, where a former player used to work.

Crewe Alexandra are named after Princess Alexandra, who later became queen as wife of King Edward VII. Ma'am-a Mia!

GUNS AND GLASS

Two big English clubs are named after buildings: Arsenal and Crystal Palace. An arsenal is where military weapons are made and stored. The Royal Arsenal in Woolwich, south London, used to be where the British armed forces kept their machinery and ammunition. In 1886, workers there started a football team called Royal Arsenal. It later changed its name to Woolwich Arsenal, and when the club moved to north London it dropped the Woolwich part. Now the most lethal weapons at Arsenal are its strikers!

The Crystal Palace used to be one of the most stunning buildings in Britain. Made of glass and cast iron and the size of about eleven football pitches, it was built in 1851 to host the Great Exhibition, a festival in Hyde Park, London, to showcase objects brought from all over the world. After the festival ended, the palace was taken down and rebuilt in Sydenham Hill, a park in south London. In order to attract visitors, the building's owners started a football team in 1905 and called it Crystal Palace. The building burnt down in 1936, but the name has proved indestructible. Not only is the area around Sydenham Hill still called Crystal Palace, but the football team is now the pride of south London!

LOTS OF HAM

Once upon a time, more than a thousand years ago, somewhere in the middle of England, there was a village on some high land.

It was called Heantun because in Old English, the language spoken at the time, the words *heah* and *tun* meant "high" and "village".

The king of England, Ethelred the Unready, gave Heantun to a noble woman called Wulfrun, when it became known as Wulfrun's Heantun.

The village grew and grew and is now known as … Wolverhampton.

Yes, the city owes its name not to a pack of wolves, but to a posh woman called Wulfrun!

Old English was spoken in Britain between around 400 and 1100 AD and its words were used in the original versions of many place names. For example, why do you think so many towns have got the word "ham" in them? No, it's not because they used to be pig farms! It's because many places used to be called *ham*, which is Old English for "village", or *hamm*, which is Old English for "land hemmed in by water or marsh".

Old English came in many dialects, such as Anglian, and was influenced by other ancient languages, like Old Norse. These languages may not be spoken any more, but we can see traces of them in the words we use now.

Let's use YE OLDE FOOTBALLE SCHOOLE DICTIONARYE to see how some of England's main football towns got their names and why.

Aston Villa
Meaning: The villa in the east village

Why: From "east" and the Old English *tun* (Aston) and because in the 1700s there was a grand house there (Villa)

Blackburn
Meaning: Black stream

Why: From the Old English *blaec*, meaning "black" or "dark", and *burna*, meaning "stream"

Brighton & Hove
Meaning: Beorhthelm's farm (Brighton) and Hood-shaped hill (Hove)

Why: From Beorhthelm, the Old English *tun* and *hufe*, meaning "a hood"

Burnley
Meaning: Brown wood (or brown clearing)

Why: From *brun*, the Old English for "brown/dark-coloured", and *leah*, for a "wood" or "clearing"

Chelsea
Meaning: Chalk landing place

Why: From *cealc*, meaning "chalk" in Old English, and *hyd*, Old English for "landing place" or "wharf"

Derby
Meaning: Deer farm

Why: From *djur*, Old Norse for "animal", and *by*, Old Norse for "farm"

Everton
Meaning: Wild boar farm

Why: From *eofor*, Old English for "wild boar", and *tun* for "farm"

Fulham
Meaning: Fulla's hemmed-in land

Why: From Fulla and the Old English *hamm*

Leicester

Meaning: Town of the Ligore

Why: From the Celtic tribal name Ligore and the Old English *ceaster*, meaning "town"

Liverpool

Meaning: Muddy pool

Why: From *lifer*, Old English for "thick, muddy water", and *pol*, a "pool" or "creek"

Manchester

Meaning: Town of the breast-shaped hill

Why: From *mamm*, meaning "breast", or "breast-shaped hill" in Primitive Welsh, and the Old English *ceaster*

Nottingham

Meaning: Village of Snot's people

Why: From the Saxon chieftain called Snot, and *-ingas*, Old English for "the people of", and the Old English *ham*

Southampton

Meaning: The south farm on hemmed-in land

Why: From the Old English *hamm* and *tun*

Stoke

Meaning: Place

Why: From *stoc*, the Old English for "place"

Tottenham

Meaning: Totta's village, or Totta's hemmed-in land

Why: From Totta and either the Old English *ham* or *hamm*

Watford

Meaning: Hunting ford

Why: From *wad*, Old English for "hunting", and *ford*, "a small river"

West Ham

Meaning: West hemmed-in land

Why: From the Old English *hamm*

SILLYVILLE

Britain is full of places with funny names. Here are some of our favourites:

- Great Snoring, Norfolk
- Brokenwind, Aberdeenshire
- Nether Wallop, Hampshire
- Puddletown, Dorset
- Barton in the Beans, Leicestershire

ENGLISH QUIZ

1. What product used to be docked at Chelsea, which gave the place its name?

a) Chocolate
b) Cheese
c) Chalk
d) Chickpeas

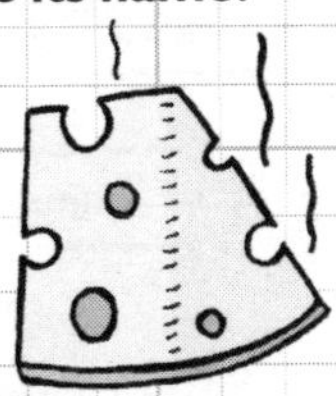

2. What is the nickname of Bristol Rovers, which is also the old meaning of the team name?

a) The Bristols
b) The Land Rovers
c) The Pirates
d) The Hounds

3. An inhabitant of Wolverhampton is called ...

a) A wolf
b) A wolverine
c) A wulfrunian
d) A wolverinian

4. What was Crystal Palace's original nickname, before it changed to the Eagles?

a) The Window Cleaners
b) The Glaziers
c) The Crystals
d) The Glassicos

5. The home stand at Liverpool is called the Kop. Where does the name come from?

a) A hill in South Africa where many local soldiers died during the Boer War
b) The Merseyside police building
c) A corner shop near Anfield where fans bought KitKats for the game
d) An abbreviation of K-pop, the favourite musical style of the club's founders

Friday
Lesson 1+2

PSYCHOLOGY

Let's start this lesson with a famous riddle.

A father and son are in a car crash. The father is killed. The son is rushed to hospital. The duty surgeon says: "I can't treat the boy. He's my son."

How is this possible?

Think about the answer for a few seconds before you read on.

For many people, this riddle is totally baffling. How on earth can the father be about to operate on the son if we know he is dead?

In fact, the answer is simple. The surgeon is not the boy's father, she is the boy's mum!

If you instantly thought that the surgeon was the mum, we applaud you. Congratulations! Most people, however, make the initial assumption that the surgeon is a man. While it is true that a lot of surgeons are men, many surgeons are women, of course.

A preconceived opinion about a person or a situation is called a bias. This lesson is all about **unconscious bias** – that is, when we make these unfair assumptions without realizing – in life and in football. If you assume something without thinking clearly about it, you could be wrong! Right?

A SLICE OF THE PROFITS

Here's our first tale of an assumption we make in daily life. At the school fete, Alex was selling cake at £1 a slice. But no one was buying.

Ben set up a stall right next to Alex selling cake at £3 a slice. And guess what? Everyone started buying Alex's £1 slices!

This is because if we see two similar-looking items priced differently, we assume the cheaper one is a bargain and are more likely to buy it. But if we see the price of one item on its own, it is hard to know whether it is good value or not.

Shops use this technique all the time. They will often display the most expensive items very prominently because this makes everything else look cheap by comparison. A pair of £100 football boots may sound expensive, but positioned in the window next to a £300 pair, they look like a steal.

The lesson here is that our minds are easily fooled – especially by people who are trying to sell us stuff. We always need to be on our guard: we cannot assume that a pair of boots (or a slice of cake) is a bargain, just because it's cheaper than another. Maybe both are expensive!

COMPARE THE MARKET
CAKE €1 per SLICE
CAKE €3 per SLICE
CAKE €1 per SLICE

YELLOW PERIL

In our second tale, Ben went to a shop to buy a pair of shoes.

He noticed that all the staff were wearing the same bright yellow trainers.

He asked if they were on sale and the salesperson said: "We only have one pair left because they are so popular!"

What did Ben do?

He bought the trainers, of course! Most people prefer to buy things that they know other people have bought. We like to feel that our decisions are backed up by the decisions of others.

In other words, just because other people think something is good, we assume that it *is* good. But here's a thought – maybe other people are all wrong! Maybe those yellow trainers are overpriced, badly made and horribly ugly.

Although it's tempting to follow the crowd, we should always pause for a moment and think for ourselves.

THINK TWICE

When we are presented with a piece of information, often we have two reactions to it.

Our first reaction is instant. It's a gut feeling. But this reaction is often full of mistaken assumptions. This can be the time when unconscious bias kicks in.

Our second reaction is one we get from reflection, by thinking about the information carefully and by realizing that our assumptions may be wrong.

Football fans do this all the time. Here we'll investigate some common assumptions in the game.

COMMON ASSUMPTION 1

Fact: Your team has signed a Brazilian.
Initial reaction: Great! They will be able to do amazing dribbles and tricks.
Considered reaction: Maybe they won't.
Assumption unpacked: Brazilians like Neymar, Philippe Coutinho and Roberto Firmino have incredible skills and they overshadow our image of what Brazilian footballers are like. When we hear about a new Brazilian we cannot help but associate them with their famous countrymen. But there are many Brazilian players and lots of them are unflashy defenders.

COMMON ASSUMPTION 2

Fact: Smith just missed a penalty. Should a team-mate take the next one?

Initial reaction: Yes!

Considered reaction: Maybe not.

Assumption unpacked: We all have short memories. If Smith missed the last penalty, we might rush to think that Smith is not a good penalty taker. But maybe Smith has taken 100 penalties before this one and scored them all. Surely the best person to take the next penalty is … Smith?

COMMON ASSUMPTION 3

Fact: Rovers beat United 1–0 in the Cup

Initial reaction: Rovers are the best team!

Considered reaction: It might have been a fluke.

Assumption unpacked: In football the best team does not always win. Unpredictability is one of the things that makes games so thrilling to watch. Just say Rovers scored a flukey goal but that 95 per cent of the game was played in their own half and they had no other chances on goal compared to United's 30 chances. We often rewrite history backwards – once you know the result, then you remember the game with that knowledge in mind. But sometimes the result is just not a fair reflection of what happened.

COMMON ASSUMPTION 4

Fact: Your club is choosing between two goalkeepers. You've heard that one is 1.9m and one is 1.6m.

Initial reaction: Pick the taller one!

Considered reaction: Height isn't everything.

Assumption unpacked: Fans tend to think that taller keepers are better keepers. But height is not the only factor in a goalkeeper's skill-set. Arm reach, shoulder flexibility and jump strength determine the height at which a goalkeeper can catch the ball, not just how tall they are with both feet on the ground. Other goalkeeping skills include good anticipation, bravery, peripheral vision, safe hands, communication and organizational skills. The shorter goalkeeper could be the better option.

COMMON ASSUMPTION 5

Fact: Your club is choosing between two coaches. One has experience of the league and the other doesn't. Do you want your club to hire the one with experience?

Initial reaction: Yes!

Considered reaction: Familiarity doesn't breed success.

Assumption unpacked: Our brains are programmed to think that being familiar with a task will make us better at it. But that's not necessarily the case. Studies have shown that having previous knowledge of a league makes NO difference to a coach's performance in that league.

MEN ARE NOT THE ONLY COACHES

Whenever a British football club changes its coach, a list of replacement names is put forward, usually made up of only men. The British football world is guilty of assuming that only men make good coaches. But this assumption is not true! Hardly any women have been appointed as head coaches, although those that have been, like Corinne Diacre, who spent three successful years at French Ligue 2 club Clermont, and Chan Yuen Ting, who won the Hong Kong first division title at Eastern, have done extremely well. Clubs are missing opportunities to improve their team by not appointing qualified women to senior positions. We hope this changes!

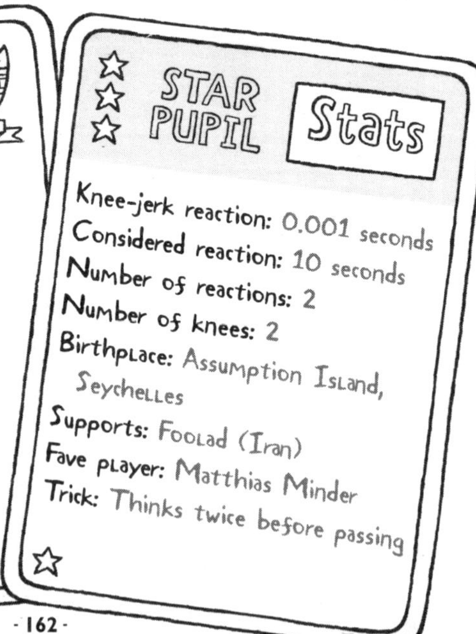

PSYCHOLOGY QUIZ

1. What nationality is Neymar?

a) Brazilian
b) Argentine
c) Dutch
d) Colombian

2. What is the word for having an assumption based on your experience or environment?

a) Justice
b) Head-mind
c) Bias
d) Guesswork

3. At what speed can nerves shoot messages from your brain to your muscles to process a thought?

a) 30 miles per hour
b) 100 miles per hour
c) 250 miles per hour
d) 400 miles per hour

4. What percentage of penalties are scored on average?

a) 50 per cent
b) 66 per cent
c) 78 per cent
d) 90 per cent

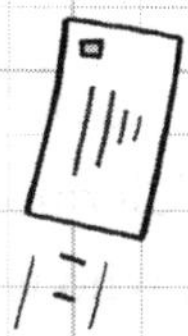

5. What did Mexico's most-capped goalkeeper Jorge Campos stand on to make himself look taller in team photos?

a) A ladder
b) The ball
c) The coach
d) The mascot

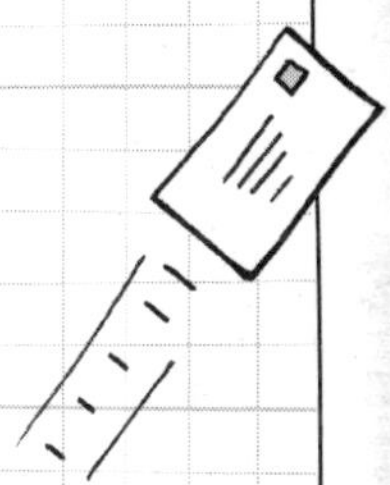

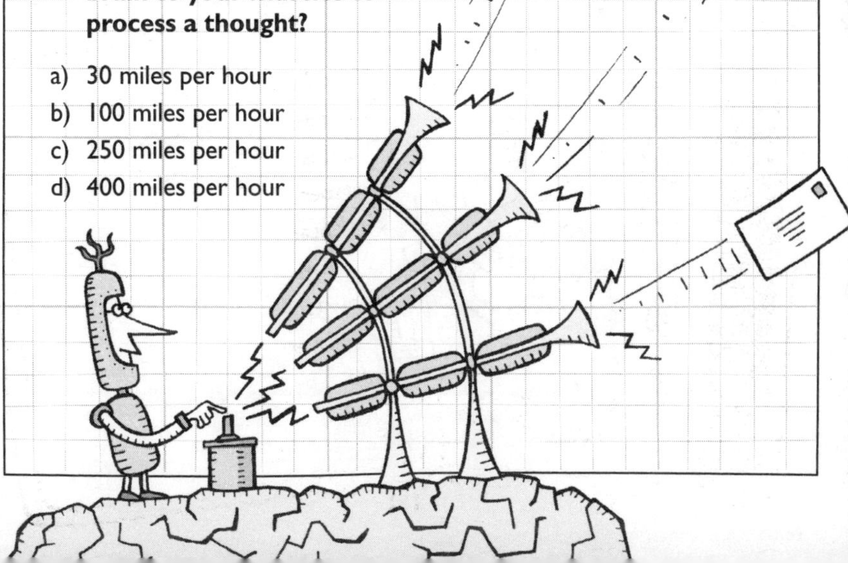

Friday
Lesson 3+4
POLITICS
What do ravens wear on their heads?
A Cro-at!
So I went for breakfast in a Yugoslavian restaurant.
What did they Serb you?
The full Montenegro!
AB
BL

Today we're off to visit the Balkans, an area of Southern Europe rich in football history. In the Balkans, they certainly *kan* play ball! We're going to look at six countries: Serbia, Croatia, Slovenia, North Macedonia, Montenegro and Bosnia and Herzegovina. (Sharp-eyed readers may have counted seven countries, but Bosnia and Herzegovina is ONE country and not two. Confusing!)

Until the early 1990s all these countries were a single country: Yugoslavia. It used to be known as the Brazil of Europe because it produced so many skilful players. In this lesson we're going to discover the role football had in the break-up of Yugoslavia and find out more about the region and its politics. Don't balk at the chance!

Are you ready? You go first! No, Yugo!

THE BIRTH OF YUGOSLAVIA

The people who live in Eastern Europe are collectively known as Slavs. In 1918 the people living in the southern part of this area decided to form a country called Yugoslavia, meaning "The Land of the South Slavs".

The idea of this new country was a noble one. For hundreds of years this area had been invaded and fought over by foreign empires, so the groups who lived here – Serbs, Croats, Bosnians, Slovenes and others – decided to come together. After all, they had a lot in common, such as similar languages, customs and geography. Southern Slavs United!

Yugoslavia had always loved football. The national team took part in the first ever World Cup in 1930, coming fourth. They won the football gold medal at the 1960 Olympics and were runner-up in the Euros in 1960 and 1968. The country's two biggest clubs, Red Star Belgrade and Dinamo Zagreb, were famous across Europe, and in 1991 Red Star won the European Cup (the forerunner of the Champions League) with a team made up almost entirely of Yugoslavs.

On 4 May 1980, Hajduk Split were hosting Red Star Belgrade in a top-of-the-table clash in the Yugoslavian league, when news came through that President Tito, who had been the leader of the country since 1953, had died. Players started weeping on the pitch and the 50,000 fans started singing songs praising Tito to express their grief.

Without a strong and popular leader like Tito to keep the peace, in the following years the friendships between Yugoslavia's different ethnic groups started to turn sour, especially between Serbs and Croats.

Belgrade is the capital of Serbia, and Zagreb is the capital of Croatia. The rivalry between fans of Red Star and Dinamo helped push the country into war.

THE KICK THAT CHANGED THE WORLD

In May 1990, a Yugoslav league match between Dinamo Zagreb and Red Star Belgrade erupted into a riot. Fans threw stones and seats, ripped up the hoardings and attacked each other with knives. Police responded to the violence with batons and tear gas. One of Dinamo's players even karate-kicked a policeman. That's not what we mean by an attacking midfielder!

The football riot was a defining moment in the history of Yugoslavia. It showed that simmering tensions between Yugoslavs could easily spill into violence. A year after that match Croats and Serbs were properly at war.

BALKAN BREAK-UP

The war between Croats and Serbs quickly spread to include Yugoslavia's other ethnic groups. Each side was fighting to establish their own independent countries. In the end Yugoslavia broke up into six different nations. The **Balkan War** of the 1990s claimed an estimated 140,000 lives, making it the bloodiest conflict in Europe since the Second World War.

The war also had an effect on football. The Yugoslavia national team was banned from Euro 1992 because of the war. That same year FIFA recognized Croatia as an independent football nation, and in the following years it recognized the teams from all the other former Yugoslav republics. Croatia qualified for its first World Cup in 1998 and came third.

Children born in the Balkans in the 1980s and 1990s grew up at a time when bombs, snipers and grenades were part of daily life. But that didn't stop many of them becoming brilliant footballers, like Luka Modrić who won the Ballon D'Or in 2018. Players from Serbia, Croatia, Slovenia, North Macedonia, Montenegro and Bosnia and Herzegovina have all played in the Premier League in recent years.

We think that if all these countries were allowed to field a single team like they used to, it might well be the best in the world!

Now the war is over, the Balkan region has become a popular tourist destination. Turn over for the Football School tour!

CROATIA

Population: 4 million
Year of independence: 1991
Capital: Zagreb
Top teams: Dinamo Zagreb, Hajduk Split
Star player: Luka Modrić

Football fact: The Croatia kit features red-and-white checks, the national symbol which covers the shield of the country's coat of arms. It dates back to the tenth century when legend has it that King Držislav, captured by the Doge (Duke) of Venice, won a chess match to gain freedom. He then put the chessboard on his coat of arms. Check them out!

Country fact: The region of Dalmatia, along the western coast of Croatia, is where William Shakespeare set his play *Twelfth Night*. It's also where Dalmatians, a breed of dog famous for its spots, first came from! Good spot!

SERBIA

Population: 7 million
Year of independence: 2006
Capital: Belgrade
Top teams: Red Star Belgrade, Partizan Belgrade
Star player: Aleksandar Mitrović
Football fact: Red Star Belgrade is the only former Yugoslav club to win the European Cup, beating French side Marseille on penalties in 1991. The derby match between Red Star and Belgrade neighbours Partizan is one of the fiercest in world football.
Country fact: Serbia is one of the world's biggest producers of raspberries. The town of Arilje hosts a festival called the Days of the Raspberry when competitions are held to find the sweetest raspberry and the tastiest raspberry cake – but luckily not who can blow the loudest raspberry!

BOSNIA AND HERZEGOVINA

Population: 3.5 million

Year of independence: 1992

Capital: Sarajevo

Top teams: FK Sarajevo, Željezničar

Star player: Miralem Pjanić

Football fact: Vedad Ibišević scored the goal that qualified Bosnia and Herzegovina for its first ever World Cup in 2014. He had escaped the war aged seven with his family, living in a house with five other families. He later moved to Switzerland and the USA before returning to Europe to turn professional.

Country fact: Bosnia makes up 80 per cent of the country and hosts the capital city Sarajevo. Herzegovina, a hilly region in the south, makes up the remaining 20 per cent. It is home to the sixteenth-century bridge Stari Most, one of the country's most iconic landmarks.

SLOVENIA

Population: 2 million
Year of independence: 1992
Capital: Ljubljana
Top teams: NK Maribor, Olimpija Ljubljana
Star player: Jan Oblak
Football fact: Slovenia has a habit of producing great goalkeepers: Samir Handanovič played for Inter Milan, Vid Belec for Sampdoria and Jan Oblak, one of the best goalkeepers in the world, played in two Champions League finals for Atlético Madrid. His father Matjaz was an amateur goalkeeper and Jan was scouted by Olimpija when practising in goal during half-time of one of his dad's games. Handy!
Country fact: Bee-keeping is one of Slovenia's oldest and proudest traditions – and one of the country's most popular hobbies. Slovenian bees produce about 2,000 tonnes of honey a year. Un-bee-lievable!

NORTH MACEDONIA

Population: 2 million

Year of independence: 1991

Capital: Skopje

Top teams: FK Vardar, Shkëndija

Star player: Goran Pandev

Football fact: Darko Pančev is seen as Macedonia's greatest ever player. He scored the winning penalty when Red Star Belgrade beat Marseille in the 1991 European Cup final. But after one bad season at Inter Milan, he was voted the worst Serie A player ever. Harsh!

Country fact: Alexander the Great, one of history's most famous military leaders, was a Macedonian who founded more than twenty cities which now bear his name (including the Egyptian port city of Alexandria). If only the national team had him as coach!

MONTENEGRO

Population: 650,000
Year of independence: 2006
Capital: Podgorica
Top team: FK Budućnost
Star player: Dejan Savićević
Football fact: Montenegro captain Mirko Vučinić had a strange way of celebrating goals. When he scored the winner against Switzerland in 2010, he ran to the fans and celebrated by taking off his shorts and putting them on his head – showing the whole stadium his white Y-fronts! He was booked by the referee – what a pants celebration!
Country fact: Montenegro is home to the Stara Maslina, one of the world's oldest olive trees, thought to be over 2,000 years old. One side of the tree is burnt, with historians unsure whether it was struck by lightning or burned after a local card game got out of hand. Sounds in-tree-guing!

DŽAJIĆ THE MAGIC DRAGAN

Dragan Džajić made more appearances than anyone else for the Yugoslavia national team. A talented left-winger, he played in the side that reached the final of the 1968 Euros, scoring the winner against England in the semi-final. The British press called him "the magic Dragan" and Pelé said, "He is the Balkan miracle – a real wizard." Džajić won five league titles with Red Star Belgrade and was helping the coach when they won the 1991 European Cup. The Serbian football federation named Džajić their best ever player to mark UEFA's 50th birthday. Sorcerer!

POLITICS QUIZ

1. Why does Croatia's home jersey have a chequerboard on it?

a) Snakes and ladders was too complicated to design.
b) It comes from the coat of arms after an ancient king won a chess match to gain his freedom.

c) A local restaurant lent the team some tablecloths to wear for its first ever match.
d) Croatia's first captain, Checko Zeckic, won the Draughts World Cup and insisted the team wore the pattern.

2. Yugoslavia was banned from the 1992 Euros because of the war. Which country replaced them at the last minute and went on to become champions?

a) Sweden
b) Portugal
c) Denmark
d) Uruguay

3. Montenegro takes its name from two Venetian words which translate as what?

a) Black mountain
b) Yellow sand
c) Green olive
d) Orange orange

4. What international youth team did Bosnia and Herzegovina midfielder Miralem Pjanić play for?

a) England
b) Bosnia and Herzegovina
c) Croatia
d) Luxembourg

5. Former Yugoslav defender Siniša Mihajlović played for Roma and Inter Milan before coaching six Italian teams and the Serbia national team. What Serie A record does he hold in Italy?

a) Most red cards shown
b) Hardest shot ever taken
c) First non-goalkeeper to save a penalty
d) Most free kicks scored

Friday
Lesson 5

MAGIC

Roll up, roll up!

Today's afternoon activity is magic club.

Magic is a type of entertainment in which a person – the magician – performs seemingly impossible feats, like making a coin vanish or a rabbit appear out of a hat. When you see a magician do a good trick, you can't quite figure out how it's done and it creates a sense of wonder and amazement.

Football is also a type of entertainment that inspires awe and disbelief, especially when you see a player perform a particularly skilful move. That's why players with amazing technique are sometimes called magicians or wizards. They seem to be doing something that defies the natural order of things.

In this week's final lesson, we're going to learn some magic tricks and some football tricks. We'll discover that both footballers and magicians rely on the same methods.

Let's tap our magic wand to find out what they are!

AND IN A PUFF OF SMOKE...

Welcome to Football School Magic Club!

The rules of magic club are that you never tell anyone else what happens here. Before we start, please sign the statement below.

FOOTBALL SCHOOL MAGIC CLUB

I, the great and mysterious ...., promise never ever to knowingly disclose the secrets contained within these pages.

I promise to look after my top hat, black suit, waistcoat and cape and keep my magic wand under my bed.

I promise to be kind to all rabbits.

My magic word is ....

Signed ....

TRICKY CHARACTERS

Magic comes in many forms. There's **close-up magic**, in which a magician performs tricks with objects like coins, cards and ropes, right in front of an audience. There's **stage magic**, in which a magician is on a stage and often uses assistants and large props. And there's **mentalism**, in which a magician makes you believe he or she can control your thoughts. Typical things magicians like to do include:

- Making things disappear and then reappear, like coins, humans and even buildings.
- Escaping from being tied up in chains, sometimes hanging upside down or in a locked box.
- Making predictions that seem impossible to know in advance – such as which card an audience member has chosen from a deck – but which turn out to be true.

Magicians use a mixture of techniques to successfully perform their tricks, of which the two most important are **misdirection** and **sleight-of-hand**.

LIGHTS, CAMERA, DISTRACTION

Alex and Ben are having lunch in the Football School canteen. Ben's phone is on the table.

Alex says: "Look! Do you see that mark on the wall?"

Ben turns around to look at the mark on the wall and Alex quickly takes Ben's phone without him noticing.

This type of deception is called misdirection. Alex is making Ben look in one direction so that Ben does not see what is happening in the other direction.

Magicians rely on this technique, which works because humans cannot look two ways at once. If a magician gets an audience to focus on, say, their left hand, they will be able to do something with their right hand that the audience will not see.

The role of the magic wand is to aid misdirection. When a magician uses a wand, the audience's eyes will naturally follow the hand with the wand, which allows the magician to use their other hand to do the trick.

The best magicians are able to misdirect you without you realizing that you are being misdirected.

FAB FINGERS AND TALENTED TOES

Sleight-of-hand is the name given to the delicate finger skills magicians rely on for many tricks, such as the ability to effortlessly move around a coin between your fingers or to hide a ball in your palm. Many card tricks are based on sleight-of-hand, such as the ability to shuffle the pack in special ways or to pick or replace a card without the audience noticing. These skills can take years to perfect.

Football tricks also rely on a combination of misdirection and amazing motor skills, although footballers use every part of the body apart from the arms, hands and fingers. Not sleight-of-hand, it's sleight-of-foot!

If you want to be a football magician, we've got some tricks for you in the following pages. But remember, whether it's magic or football, tricks require lots and lots of practice to become seamless. Best of luck!

MAGIC TRICK 1: HOW TO MAKE A COIN APPEAR IN YOUR HAND

Method: Sleight-of-hand

Step 1: First, you need to learn how to "palm" a coin, which means to keep it in your palm without anyone realizing it is there. To do this, place a coin in the middle of your right hand (if you are right-handed), or your left (if you are left-handed). Cup your hand slightly so the coin is lodged between the base of your thumb and the top of your palm. When you turn your hand over, the coin should stay in position. Get used to moving your hand around with the coin in your palm.

Step 2: Show your audience your other (empty) hand and tell them you will make a coin appear in it. Open your palm to convince them that there is no coin there, and then position your hand with your knuckles facing your audience and your thumb touching your forefinger.

Step 3: Say your magic word and pass your coin hand over your empty hand in the most natural way possible. When the palm of your coin hand is over your empty hand, release the coin by loosening the thumb muscle in your coin hand. The coin will fall between the thumb and forefinger into the palm of your empty hand. You need to make sure that your empty hand is at a slight angle, so that the coin falls straight into it. Because your hand is moving when you release the coin, this will take time to master.

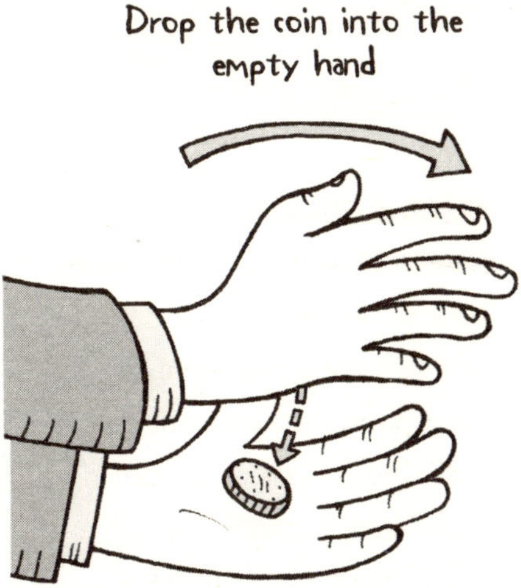

Step 4: Open your hand to reveal the coin.

How it works: The audience does not realize you are hiding, releasing and catching a coin with your hands.

MAGIC TRICK 2: HOW TO MOVE A PENCIL WITHOUT TOUCHING IT

Method: Misdirection

Step 1: Make sure the radio is on. Don't tell your audience, but background noise is needed for this trick! Announce that you are going to move a pencil using static electricity. Show your audience the pencil and place it on the table.

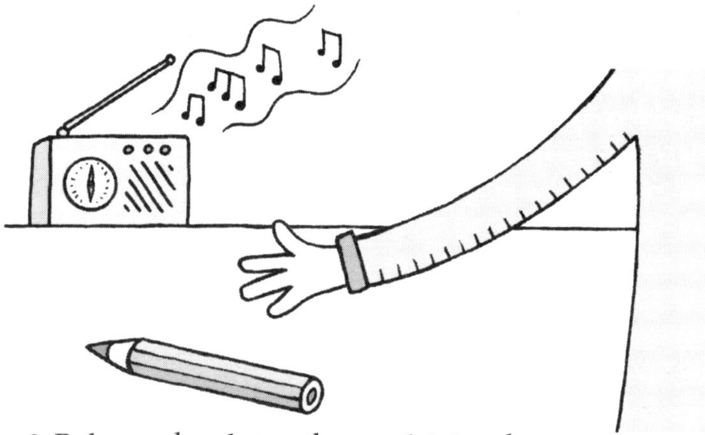

Step 2: Rub your hands together, explaining that this is what is making the static electricity.

Step 3: Move your hands towards the pencil and at the same time lower your face and blow silently down at the table. The pencil will roll away as if propelled by static electricity, but it's really the air current that's moving it!

How it works: Everyone is looking at your hands in order to check you are not touching the pencil. No one is looking at your mouth, so they don't see that you are blowing.

MAGIC TRICK 3: HOW TO FOOL A FRIEND

Method: Misdirection and sleight-of hand

Step 1: You'll need a paper clip and five playing cards. Make sure one is a queen. Hold the five cards together as illustrated, and show them face up to a friend. Make it clear that the queen is the middle one.

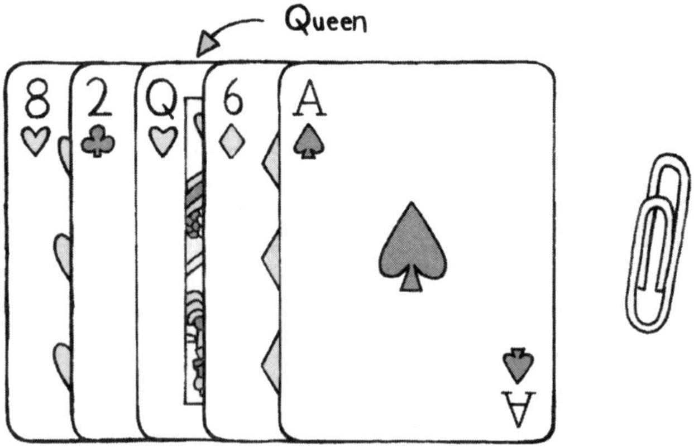

Step 2: Turn the cards over as illustrated. Ask your friend to place the paper clip on the queen.

Step 3: Make sure you are holding the cards tight together so that when your friend clips the queen, they clip all the cards under the queen too.

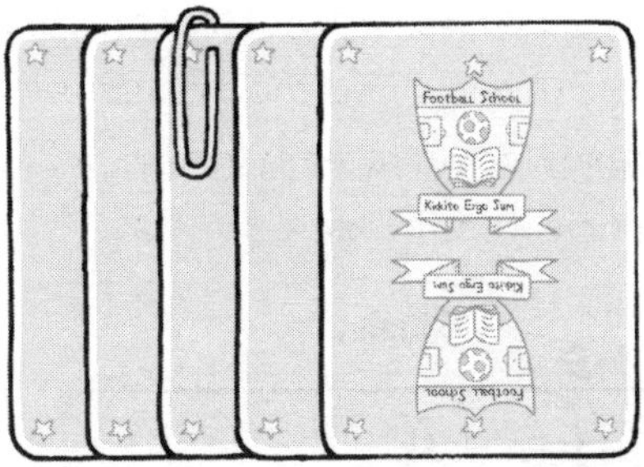

Step 4: When you turn the cards over you will see that your friend has not clipped the queen, but the fifth card along.

How it works: There are two types of misdirection here. First, your friend is directed to clip three cards, rather than just the queen. Second, the positioning of the cards is misleading, causing your friend to make a mistake. The queen is the middle card, so it makes sense to clip the middle card. However, the piece of middle card that is visible is not actually in the middle of the five cards when spread out. Even though they think they are clipping in the middle, they are not. The sleight-of-hand is making sure that you hold the cards tight so your friend clips all the cards.

FOOTBALL TRICK 1: ZIDANE ROULETTE

Made famous by: Zinédine Zidane (France)

What it is: Player performs a 360-degree turn while running forward.

Useful for: Finding space away from an opponent.

Why it works: Turning your back on the defender surprises them and the quick turn straight after adds more confusion. That's before they've even realized the ball has gone past them!

How to do it:

1. Dribble towards opponent, plant your right foot on top of the ball and simultaneously hop in a 180-spin to the left.

2. As the ball moves back, place your right foot on the ground (in front of the ball) and plant your left foot on top of the ball.

3. Complete the 360-spin while dragging the ball as you complete your turn.

Top tip: Practise this in slow motion first.

FOOTBALL TRICK 2: FOOLING THE KEEPER

Made famous by: Eden Hazard (Belgium), Mario Balotelli (Italy) and others

What it is: Kicking the ball to the left when your body language suggests you will kick it to the right (or vice versa).

Useful for: Scoring penalties.

Why it works: Tricks the goalkeeper into diving to one side, so you can score on the other side.

How to do it:

1. When you take a penalty, look at one of the corners of the goal when you make your runup. Your body language will make the keeper think that you will aim for that corner.

2. Just before you strike the ball, watch the goalkeeper to see the direction of their dive.

3. If the goalkeeper moves towards the direction that you were looking at, quickly switch your body angle and aim for the other corner. If the keeper is trying to out-think you and dives to the corner that you were not looking at, then carry on as normal and shoot to the original corner. With practice, you should score every time!

Top tip: Practise taking penalties while switching your eye-line from corner to goalkeeper.

FOOTBALL TRICK 3: CRUYFF TURN

Made famous by: Johan Cruyff (Netherlands)

What it is: You look like you are going one way, when all of a sudden you go the other way.

Useful for: Turning away from danger.

Why it works: Fools the opponent into going the wrong way.

How to do it:

1. Pull back your right foot and pretend to pass down the pitch.

2. Hold the foot over the ball and draw it behind your standing leg.

3. Spin 180 degrees, shift weight to left foot, and run with the ball in the opposite direction.

Top tip: Practise keeping your balance while flicking the ball behind your standing leg.

REAL MAGIC

Former Arsenal player Santi Cazorla is nicknamed *El Mago* or "The Magician", in Spanish. When he rejoined the club where he began his career, Villarreal, he was presented to fans by Spain's top magician Yunke, who placed an empty glass tube on the pitch which he filled with smoke. When the smoke cleared, Cazorla was standing there. Hocus toe-cus!

MAGIC QUIZ

1. What is the term for trying to get someone to look the wrong way?

a) Indirection
b) Wrongdirection
c) Misdirection
d) Onedirection

2. What is the name of the magician who was famous for his amazing escape acts?

a) Harry Styles
b) Harry Houdini
c) Harry Redknapp
d) Harry Kane

3. Spanish midfielder David Silva is known by the popular nickname of *El Mago*. What does it mean?

a) The Illusionist
b) The Witch
c) The Magician
d) The Mentalist

4. The word feint, meaning a false attack, comes from which activity?

a) Fencing
b) Fainting
c) Farting
d) Flying

5. What name is given to the international society set up in 1905 to promote the art of magic?

a) Now You See Us
b) The Merlin Club
c) The Magic Circle
d) The Conjurors' Class

Now you see us!
Now you don't!
Yes, it's the end of the book.
Ladies and gentlemen, you've been a great audience!
It's been magical!
We've travelled all over the world – and to outer space.
We've met a king in Japan and a queen in Crewe.
Football royalty!
And the striker from Montenegro who celebrates goals in his underwear.
He's pants!
We've learned about strange sports, like spitting fruit stones.
Cherry good!

About new technologies, like virtual and augmented reality.
For real!
And the British monarch who inspired the Champions League anthem.
Champion!
We know the club named after wild boar.
The player trapped underground for 69 days.
And we learned that failure is important for future success.
Group hug!
We've looked at the history of clocks and watches.
Talking of watches, we're out of time!
Until next time!
Peeeeeeeep!

QUIZ ANSWERS

BIOLOGY
1. d
2. b
3. a
4. b
5. a

MUSIC
1. a
2. b
3. b
4. a
5. c

MODERN LANGUAGES
1. c
2. a
3. b
4. d
5. b

COMPUTER SCIENCE
1. b
2. a
3. d
4. c
5. b

MATHS
1. c
2. c
3. c
4. b
5. d

PHILOSOPHY
1. d
2. c
3. b
4. b
5. d

SCHOOL TRIP

1. b
2. c
3. b
4. d
5. c

PSYCHOLOGY

1. a
2. c
3. c
4. c
5. b

HISTORY

1. a
2. d
3. c
4. b
5. b

POLITICS

1. b
2. c
3. a
4. d
5. d

PSHE

1. a
2. d
3. a
4. a
5. a

MAGIC

1. c
2. b
3. c
4. a
5. c

ENGLISH

1. c
2. c
3. c
4. b
5. a

ACKNOWLEDGEMENTS

We love the number four! There are four points of a compass, four seasons in every year, four limbs on the human body, four years between each World Cup and four cheeses on Ben's favourite pizza. Now there are four seasons of Football School! So we want to give FOUR CHEERS to our ingenious illustrator Spike!

The four-midable backroom staff at Walker Books push us to our peak writing performance. We are grateful to all of them: head coach Daisy Jellicoe, sporting director Denise Johnstone-Burt, tactical visionary Laurelie Bazin; and also Josh Alliston, Rosi Crawley, Jamie Hammond, Jo Humphreys-Davies, Louise Jackson, Jill Kidson, James McParland, Megan Middleton, John Moore, Rebecca Oram, Ed Ripley and Frances Taffinder.

We are four-tunate to have a great team of agents behind us: Rebecca Carter, Rebecca Folland, Kirsty Gordon, Ellis Hazelgrove, David Luxton, Zoe Nelson, Nick Waters and Rebecca Winfield.

The animal phrase examples from the Modern Languages chapter are taken from *Do You Speak Football?* by our friend Tom Williams. It's a great read and we recommend that you go out and buy it!

We would also like to thank the following experts for sharing their time and knowledge with us: Al Bennett, Rick Blaskey, Simone Blaskey, Ronan Boscher, Dr Matt Bristow and Kjell van Paridon from Anglia Ruskin University, Onofre Costa, Jon Henderson, Alex Holiga, Simon Horobin, Jenny Laurence, Hans Leitert, Jason Marantz, John McCulloch, Ian Pearson, Adam Rubin, Jim Sells, Sebastian Stanbury, Kristof Terreur, Thomas Tuchel and Richard Wiseman.

Shout out to our Star Pupils: Lucas and Mia Christenson, Akshay Jain, keepy-uppy legend Zack James, Eugene and Felix Joliot, Sonny Lampitt and Jamie Stott.

Ben would like to thank Annie for her continued inspiration and Clemmy and Bibi for their smiles, support and skills. Alex would like to thank Barnaby, Zak and Nat.

ABOUT YOUR COACHES

Alex Bellos writes for the *Guardian*. He has written several bestselling popular science books and created two mathematical colouring books. He loves puzzles.

Ben Lyttleton is a journalist, broadcaster and football consultant. He has written books about how to score the perfect penalty and what we can learn from football's best managers.

Spike Gerrell grew up loving both playing football and drawing pictures. He now gets to draw for a living. At heart, though, he will always be a central midfielder.

OUT NOW!

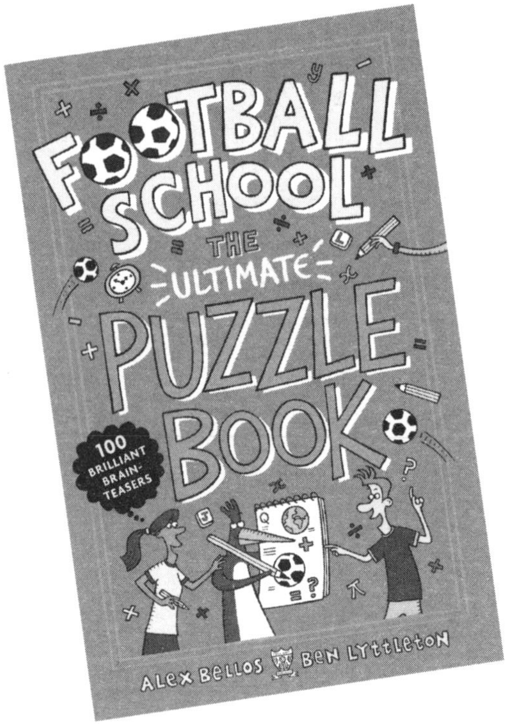
FOOTBALL SCHOOL
THE ULTIMATE
PUZZLE BOOK
100 BRILLIANT BRAIN-TEASERS
ALEX BELLOS
BEN LYTTLETON

COMING SOON!

FOOTBALL SCHOOL
EPIC HEROES
50 TRUE TALES THAT SHOOK THE WORLD
ALEX BELLOS
BEN LYTTLETON

FOOTBALL SCHOOL
FOOTBALL
SCHOOL

COLLECT THE FOOTBALL SCHOOL SERIES
FOOTBALL SCHOOL
Season 1
WHERE FOOTBALL EXPLAINS THE WORLD
FOOTBALL SCHOOL
Season 2
WHERE FOOTBALL EXPLAINS THE WORLD
FOOTBALL SCHOOL
Season 3
WHERE FOOTBALL EXPLAINS THE WORLD
FOOTBALL SCHOOL
STAR PLAYERS
50 INSPIRING STORIES OF TRUE FOOTBALL HEROES
FOOTBALL SCHOOL
THE INCREDIBLE JOKE BOOK
OVER 300 FAN-TASTIC QUESTIONS
FOOTBALL SCHOOL
THE AMAZING QUIZ BOOK
TEST YOUR WORLD CUP KNOWLEDGE!
FOOTBALL SCHOOL
EPIC HEROES
50 TRUE TALES THAT SHOOK THE WORLD
FOOTBALL SCHOOL
THE ULTIMATE PUZZLE BOOK
100 BRILLIANT BRAIN-TEASERS
ALEX BELLOS
BEN LYTTLETON

Coming soon